TRAMWAYS OF THE WORLD

TRAMWAYS
OF THE WORLD

by

J. Joyce

LONDON

IAN ALLAN

Published by Ian Allan Ltd., Shepperton, Middlesex, and printed by
A. Quick & Co. (Printers) Ltd., Oxford Road, Clacton-on-Sea, England.

Contents

Illustrations

Colour Plates
facing pages 32 and 33

Introduction

THE aim of this book is to give a glimpse of some of the world's tramways. Coverage is by no means comprehensive – the field is too wide for that – but a representative selection from different countries includes examples of particular interest, importance or strangeness.

With three exceptions – London, Manchester and Glasgow – all the tramways described are still extant and most of them look like functioning for a long time yet. The three extinct specimens are large British systems which point a contrast with those overseas.

Readers in Britain, where trams have almost completely disappeared outside museums, may be surprised to find that so many are still running in other countries. In these places the trams are not merely a survival but are often a vital part of modern city transport, sometimes with ambitious plans for future development.

I am happy to acknowledge the assistance of the many people who have helped me in the compilation of this book, including the travellers who have studied individual systems and published the results of their research. In particular I am greatly indebted to Mr W. J. Wyse, Overseas Editor of *Modern Tramway*, for reading the overseas sections, supplying additional material and photographs, and saving me from numerous errors; and to Mr G. B. Claydon for his comments on the British sections as well as for photographs.

I am also grateful to Mr T. M. Russell for details and photographs of Karachi, and to the photographers – Messrs Hugh Ballment, J. Bazin, W. A. Camwell, N. N. Forbes, Ralph Forty, J. W. Higgins, R. James, P. Malterre, A. D. Packer, J. H. Price, Thomas C. Swinney, Frits van Dam, K. J. Walker and Jan Walter – all of whom have generously waived any reproduction fees in order that royalties from the sale of this book can go to the Light Railway Transport League and the Tramway Museum Society.

J.J.

I

Rails in the World's Streets

MANY years ago a certain American town is said to have issued picture postcards of its main street showing tram rails and wires, although in real life it had never possessed such embellishments. Fearful of seeming to be left behind when this mode of transport was in vogue, it had faked the evidence to bring itself up to date. The importance attached to trams persists even today, when in numerous cities throughout the world the tracks and overhead are so much a part of the townscape that they are taken for granted. Although it may differ in detail from country to country, the tram is world-wide.

Trams appeared in New York in 1832, in Paris in 1853, in London in 1861, and within a few years streets everywhere were echoing to the clip-clop of the horse and glistening with the lines of shining rails. Cable and steam traction replaced horses in the 1880s and 1890s, while in the late 1890s and early 1900s came electric power to give a dramatic new impetus to the tram, sending it expanding in the cities and establishing itself in almost every major town.

A world that was becoming increasingly urbanised needed a system of public transport in its busy cities. Moreover, industrialisation in Britain, Europe and the United States meant a rise in the standard of living and a demand for local transport.

The industrialised nations – Great Britain, Germany and the United States – did not keep the benefits of modern life to themselves. They wanted to spread their knowledge and invest their money in other lands, and goods from Manchester, Düsseldorf and Pittsburgh were despatched to the world's markets. Capital, technical knowledge and equipment went overseas to install and operate tramways in all parts of the globe.

Trams were taken up the Nile to Khartoum, across the deserts to Beirut and Baghdad, to the swarming plains of India, to the jungles of Brazil, and across the great wall of China. Thus inspired, what town or city could lag behind?

If in the years of the boom numerous tramways seemed to be built with more optimism than business acumen, it has to be recalled that at the time there was no satisfactory alternative form of transport. Few could foresee that not so long after the electric tram had established itself the motor bus would appear as a rival. When it came, competition was frequently un-restrained, with the newcomer having the advantage of greater freedom of manoeuvre without the handicap of a substantial amount of costly fixed equipment. The result was that many tramways disappeared, although others have had a remarkable tenacity to life.

*   *   *

In Britain horse tramways came into use in the main towns in the 1870s and 1880s, to be followed in a number of places by cable and steam. The electric boom arrived around the turn of the century and the rails spread rapidly, enjoying a heyday in the years to 1914.

Ominous signs began to appear in the post-war years with the development of motor buses and trolleybuses and the need for renewal and extension. Then in the 1930s came large-scale replacement, only halted by the Second World War but resumed soon afterwards, until by the early 1960s nearly all British tramways had been swept away. There remain today only those at Blackpool, Douglas and at Crich Museum, all of them representing special uses – such as holiday traffic – rather than the urban services which the tram traditionally provided.

*   *   *

In North America the tram has disappeared almost as completely as in Britain. Canada still has streetcars in Toronto, although a new under-ground railway is being built and an existing one extended with the aim of taking traffic off the streets.

The United States was once the land of the trolley (the word 'tram' in its British sense was not normally used in America, the tramway being a 'street railway' and its vehicles 'streetcars' or 'trolleys'). Not only did practically every community of any size have its local lines, but there were far-flung interurban networks which took electric cars rushing across the countryside from town to town.

Typical interurban rolling stock comprised massive wooden-bodied vehicles about the size of British railway carriages. They came into their own when they reached the right-of-way on the edge of town where the line became almost indistinguishable from a fully-fledged railway. Speeds were high and distances long, sometimes 100 miles or more. Some services even provided restaurant facilities as well as baggage cars for express freight, but the heyday of the interurban ended with the advent of the private car and the motor lorry.

It was the private car too, together with unrestricted bus competition and the sprawl of towns into new suburbs, which spelt doom for the American city lines.

In an attempt to meet the perilous situation, trolley operators banded together to form the Electric Railway Presidents' Conference Committee and dreamed up the vehicle that was to be known by the initials of that organisation – the PCC-car. First produced in 1934, the PCC was the apotheosis of the American streetcar. Whereas the old trolley was slow, noisy and uncomfortable, the PCC was to be just the opposite.

Curvacious and streamlined, it was light in weight, dashing and comfortable, with rubber inserts in the wheels to deaden noise and vibration and give smooth running. A new type of control equipment inspired a fast glideaway start, and high-speed motors pepped up its performance so that it could challenge the private automobile.

It was a brave try, and if it did not halt the decline of American tramways it delayed the process in certain places. Moreover, although none have been built in the United States for 15 years, the PCC has had a strong influence on development elsewhere; it has spread throughout the world and its technology has been adopted in some of the countries where tramways still continue.

Nowadays American streetcars are confined to little more than the Boston system, which includes routes in subways, and suburban lines in Philadelphia, while in San Francisco the cable cars still clamber up the hills. But although electric traction in the streets has nearly gone, consideration is now being given to the introduction of new 'rapid transit' systems which would bring back rail transport to revive traffic-choked cities.

*　　　*　　　*

A glance at the rest of the world will give an idea where tramways are to be found today. Indeed there are so many that it is impossible to mention every one individually, for the tram holds sway in countless places and is likely to remain for a long time yet. Apart from anything else, the sheer physical task and cost of removing it would make it an expensive job, regardless of the fact that in numerous places it still performs its purpose well.

In Continental Europe it flourishes in many cities, notably in Germany, Holland, Belgium and Switzerland, as well as in certain towns in Scandinavia. In Russia and Eastern Europe too, tramways are widespread, helped by the fact that towns in these countries do not yet have the concentration of private cars and other traffic in their streets to hinder public transport, which can also be 'built in' to serve planned housing development.

On the other side of the world, although tramways have ceased in New Zealand, they continue in Australia in Melbourne and Brisbane. South Africa no longer has city services, but at the other end of the continent there are trams in Cairo and Alexandria. Elsewhere, South American cities still have tramways, as do those of China and Japan, the latter country in particular having vehicles of startlingly modern design.

Their survival in South America, as well as in other less-developed parts of the world, must be linked with the economic conditions in those countries. Often started with foreign capital, tramways represent substantial assets which cannot be quickly or lightly thrown away. The operators just do not have enough money available to be able to afford this.

Moreover, with a relatively low standard of living, their passengers cannot afford to pay the higher fares that would almost inevitably come with large-

scale re-equipment, whether this took the form of new trams or the introduction of replacing buses on a sufficiently lavish basis to provide comparable
capacity.

In these circumstances, therefore, it is hardly surprising that in many
cities of the world the trams remain supreme. Operators often have to keep
them running to extraordinary ages, but they appreciate their durability
and their heavy overload capacity, while the passengers appreciate the low
fares that are possible.

This indicates two characteristics which have ensured the tram a place
in overseas urban transport over the years.

First, its great carrying ability. This has not been restricted to the number
of seats in it (this has been largely a British idea) but rather to the number
of people who could be swallowed up in its capacious maw or who could
find some hold on the outside by clinging to handrails or bumpers. With a
vast overload potential, and perhaps with a string of trailers tethered on
behind, it has proved an economical crowd-shifter.

Second, its longevity. The tram has often proved almost indestructible,
and even after 40, 50 or even 60 years in the streets it has still managed to
struggle along. In the end it may have looked ludicrously old-fashioned,
and too often its long life has been its undoing by giving it a bad name and
by making it unable to compete with the modern bus.

With the raising of living standards that will come in the future, the
pattern may change. Wealthier customers, even if they cannot afford their
own personal transport (and the number of private cars will inevitably rise),
may demand a higher standard of public transport – and they will be able
to pay for it. Where modernisation has been tardy, they may welcome new
buses in place of the old trams, especially as the redevelopment of towns
and the growth of road traffic makes things more difficult for the railed
vehicles.

But in many places such a situation is a long way off, and meanwhile
the trams continue to run.

*   *   *

Concurrently there are signs that the opposite is in fact happening and
that this form of transport is enjoying a renaissance in the highly developed
lands of Western Europe.

Destruction during the war meant that drastic reconstruction of towns
and transport had to be undertaken after 1945. Sometimes the tramways
were scrapped as soon as replacing buses could be obtained. This applied
particularly in small towns where capital could not be found, where loads
were sufficiently light as to make the motor bus a more economical proposition,
or where housing development was going on beyond the old rail routes.

In other places, though, the tramways were retained. Where new streets
were laid out, new lines were 'built in' on reservations, and the city centre
was planned to incorporate them, with improved layouts, loading islands and
stations. In the suburbs routes were also placed on reservation where possible.

At the same time, improved rolling stock of modern design made its appearance. In pre-war years the typical Continental tram was a four-wheeler with one or more similar trailers. Its post-war equivalent is much larger. At first it was a roomy bogie car, then it was articulated to make it virtually two single units joined together in the middle.

These great vehicles have given a completely different aspect to the economics of operation. They can carry up to six times the number of passengers as the smaller cars but with no increase in the number of crew required. The big bogie or articulated car can carry between 150 and 300 passengers yet needs a crew of no more than two. In this case it obviously has a good lead over the bus. Indeed, with high capacity on good routes with private right-of-way, the modern tramway's competitor is not so much the bus as the railway.

This development is being seen in some cities – such as Stockholm and Hamburg – where the trams are falling before the advance of underground railways. Where the traffic to be carried is especially heavy and beyond the range of the tramway's 10,000 or 20,000 passengers an hour, and where congestion makes it imperative that public transport be removed from the streets, then surface transport is being replaced by underground railways.

But these are of course extremely costly to build. They can be afforded or justified only in the biggest cities, where traffic is heaviest and money most easily found. Elsewhere a compromise situation has to be found.

This compromise retains existing tramways by developing them so that they take on many of the characteristics and advantages of underground railways, but at only a fraction of the cost. The scheme is to put the lines below ground in the busiest central parts of the city, while in the suburbs they are – as far as possible – laid on their own right of way. The result is a light railway system, having the merits of being segregated from other traffic and yet of being easily accessible.

By this means public transport is separated from private transport, to the benefit of both. The tramways can provide a fast uninterrupted service free from the delays of traffic jams, while the streets are cleared of the load of public transport.

Plans for upgrading of this nature have been made in Brussels, The Hague, Stuttgart, Frankfurt, Essen, Munich, Düsseldorf, Cologne, Bremen and Hanover, while actual work on such schemes has started in Stuttgart, Frankfurt and Cologne. A taste of things to come is shown in the Brussels subway which is already in use but which is only a small part of a much more ambitious plan. When these schemes are completed, the result will be a fresh concept of the tram and a new lease of life for a form of transport sometimes considered obsolete.

*   *   *

Trams throughout the world can show considerable variety, from ancient to modern in nearly all shapes and sizes. Practically the only common factor in their design is that almost everywhere outside Britain they have been single-deckers. In Britain the double-decker was always typical, in direct contrast to the rest of the world, where the single-decker was virtually unchallenged.

Where the double-decker appeared overseas it was usually due to British influence – it is said that the Briton when he goes abroad takes a little bit of his native land with him. The lofty double-decker was to be found in India and South Africa, while it can still be seen in Hong Kong.

In what other ways does the overseas tram differ from the British? The fact that it is a single-decker might suggest that its capacity is lower, but unlike its British equivalent it has generally been intended to carry a large number of standing passengers. The Briton might demand a seat in his public service vehicle, but the passenger in other lands is content to stand inside the vehicle rather than wait at the stop until he can get a seat. Hence the tram may well carry a greater number standing than seated.

Further, the foreign tram often does not come singly but in whole trains. If British operators, hampered by restrictive legislation, found themselves obliged to put their passengers on the roof and run their vehicles separately, overseas operators have simply coupled two or more together. The trailer is a long-established institution, although in places it is now giving way to the large-capacity single unit. The economics of the two-car set have been undeniable – the extra car requires a crew of only one as it does not need a driver.

Again, in many places overseas there has been a healthy contempt of the dividing line between 'tramway' and 'railway'. If to the Briton the tram is something that is confined to the city street, the overseas view is more flexible. Here the tram has a remarkable quality of amphibiousness; if it is quite happy in the street, it is equally at home on its own right-of-way, either on a reservation in the centre or at the side of the road or away from the streets altogether – even under the ground. This versatility is helping it to survive where it can take on something of the character of a railway.

The modern tram overseas, too, can frequently show a standard of development that was quite unknown in its British counterpart. This is revealed not only in technical refinements like truck design, braking systems and electronic control, but in such features of operation as mechanised fare collection and passenger flow.

In Continental Europe the modern tram is commonly arranged for single-ended operation. Turning facilities are provided at each terminus, so that the car requires only one driving position and one set of controls, as well as doors on one side only. This simplifies the passenger-flow system, whereby passengers board at one doorway, pay their fare to a conductor seated at a cash desk, and alight by another doorway. The flow is speeded up by the widespread use of a 'flat fare' which is the same for any distance.

By utilising methods almost unknown in Britain, and by evolving along lines in keeping with current developments, the modern tram retains its position as a vital form of urban transport.

II

Along the Golden Mile
(Blackpool)

WHO can resist trams that take such shapes as a Mississippi paddle boat, a Wild West train, a space rocket or a hovercraft? The fact that there are still trams in Blackpool at all is strange enough to begin with. Once upon a time, when this form of transport was in vogue, they would have aroused little comment, but now that they are almost the sole survivors of their breed in Britain, the visitor may be forgiven if he gazes in wonder and is tempted on board.

And how much more so when he sees such peculiar shapes. These strange creations are the illuminated trams, built up from vehicles that have served their time in more normal guise and have been metamorphosed by the Corporation's craftsmen and bedecked with a multitude of coloured lights. When dusk falls they emerge from their hiding places in the depot and parade up and down the promenade, acting as enchanting mobile adjuncts to the background of the famous illuminations. Moreover, passengers can ride in these fairyland monsters, and how much more exciting they are than the mundane motor bus.

There are other novel aspects of the Blackpool trams. One is that for most of the way they are unlike their traditional cousins in that they do not run along the streets; instead they are segregated from other traffic on their own tracks, thus making the tramway in effect a private railway along the seafront.

This is a particularly useful point during the period of the Autumn illuminations; at this time the 'lights' attract a great conglomeration of motor cars and coaches which crawl slowly through the streets while the trams can keep moving freely along their own right of way. Indeed they are recognised as the best way of seeing the sights of the illuminations, and the fact that they can get through irrespective of other traffic partly explains why they have been retained.

Another clue to their survival is that they have the unusual merit of appearing modern. Not all the fleet, of course, takes the strange forms of the decorated cars, but the present total of about 100 looks very different from the traditional concept of the old-timer.

In the 1930s Blackpool decided to modernise its tramways when many other towns were scrapping theirs. This decision resulted in a batch of some 100 newcomers being put on the rails between 1933 and 1938 so that Blackpool's trams were up-to-date while those in other towns were old and decrepit. These modern vehicles could look forward to a long life, particularly as the seasonal nature of the traffic meant that many of them were intensively used only during the summer months. Further, their maintenance costs were by no means so high as with their older counterparts; they could work at a good profit and produce a happy financial position.

The process of keeping the fleet up to date was continued in the post-war years. Not only were the pre-war vehicles brought up to the latest standards, but in 1952 twenty-five new single-deckers were obtained, followed in 1960 by ten new trailer cars.

These trailers represent another unusual development. One tram by itself is odd enough in Britain, but two together is even more so. Although common in many parts of the world, the use of trailers has never been widespread in Britain. But with these 'trains' Blackpool was supplied with units that could carry a total of 96 passengers, very handy for coping with the holiday crowds.

For here is the salient factor in transport here. Blackpool is a holiday resort, and the main purpose of the trams in the season is not to deal with crowds of workers but with multitudes of holidaymakers. People travel here not to get to or from their work but simply for pleasure. That is why, instead of showing 'Workman' on the indicator, their trams show 'Coastal Tour'. That is why there are decorated and illuminated trams. And that is why the trams have been kept up to date so that they are as attractive to the casual traveller as the contemporary motor coach.

The trams are to be seen all the way along the promenade. The route starts at South Shore on the boundary with the neighbouring borough of Lytham St. Annes, and here there is a neatly laid out turning circle. The line begins its journey along the sea front by the South Promenade, then reaches Pleasure Beach where there is another turning circle within sight of the big dipper in the nearby amusement park.

Continuing, the route reaches the South Pier, then passes the amusement arcades, stalls and cafés of the celebrated Golden Mile before coming to the Tower and the Central Pier. It then goes on to the North Promenade and past the North Pier to a further turning circle at Little Bispham. For this entire distance of five miles the line is on its own right of way, between the seashore and the roadway, with the exception of a short length near the Central Pier where it runs along the street.

But the Promenade is not the whole of the story. Little Bispham, where the promenade and the lights and the hotels end, is not the end of the line, although many cars reverse here.

The tramway goes on, still on its own right of way, past housing estates and bungalows and through fields for several miles more until it finally reaches the fishing port and resort of Fleetwood. Here it enters the streets again to run through the town until it terminates at a loop around the

Trams have served the world's cities, from the snows of northern Europe to the heat of Asia. A wintry scene in Brussels contrasts with shirt sleeves in Delhi.

(F. van Dam; Hugh Ballment

PLATE 1

The photographs on this page illustrate some of the varieties of rolling stock on the Blackpool tramways. At the top is the 'Wild West Train,' created on the chassis of two old trams. The driver rides in the 'smoke-box' of the 'locomotive.' Second, a line-up on the Promenade, showing two open 'boat' cars, as well as double-deckers. Note the strings of lights suspended from the trolley tower. Bottom left, a two-car train at the Pleasure Beach; bottom right, a pre-war rail-coach at a 'station' on the Fleetwood Tramroad.

(J. Joyce, W. J. Wyse

PLATE 2

lighthouse by the ferry – how many other lighthouse keepers can travel to their work by tram? The total distance from South Shore to the terminus at Fleetwood is about 11 miles.

This line to Fleetwood was formerly a separate undertaking with the name of the Blackpool and Fleetwood Tramroad. It was opened in 1898 from Fleetwood to Blackpool, entering Blackpool along the promenade and then reaching the centre of the town by branching off from the seafront along Dickson Road to the present North Station. It was not until 1920 that the company was acquired by Blackpool Corporation, and soon the lines were linked up with the Corporation tracks on the promenade at Gynn Square.

The Corporation itself came earlier on the scene. Indeed it can boast that it opened the first electric street tramway in Britain, for in 1885 a line began operation along the promenade. At first the now familiar overhead wire and trolley pole were absent and the conduit system of current collection was employed instead. The conductor rails were buried beneath the tracks, and cars picked up current by means of a 'plough' passing through a slot between the running rails.

This contrivance was not too successful, as the salt water in the sea air played havoc with the insulation, while small boys had a fine game in dropping obstacles into the slot – they pushed iron hoops or wire down to touch the conductor rails and then enjoyed the fireworks. Sometimes too the sea would flood over the promenade and have the same effect of interrupting the supply. On occasion things were so bad that horses had to be called in to rescue the marooned trams.

Finally, by 1899, the conduit was given up in despair and was replaced by the overhead trolley, while in the next few years new routes were laid to serve the districts of Marton and Layton.

To the south, connection was made with neighbouring Lytham St. Annes and this municipality's cars penetrated through to Blackpool for a time before being abandoned in 1937. In Blackpool itself the tramways to Layton and along Central Drive were also closed during the 1930s, while since the war the routes to Marton, Squires Gate and North Station have also been replaced by buses, with the result that the present system comprises the promenade and Fleetwood routes.

The trams now in use have developed from the first primitive ones of 1885. One example of these pioneers still exists; it is a small four-wheel open-top double-decker, initially used on the conduit system but later fitted with a trolley pole for the overhead wire.

A later variety of rolling stock was particularly striking in appearance; this was the 'Dreadnought', an apt name for a fearsome-looking double-decker with peculiar twin stairways that seemed capable of scooping up even the most dense crowd of would-be passengers. Again one of this type has been preserved.

A revolutionary design appeared in the 1930s after it had been decided to modernise. The first was put on the road in 1933. Streamlined in a gay livery of green and cream, it was a centre-entrance single-decker with transverse upholstered seats for 48 passengers and with a partitioned cab for the driver.

Soon others of similar design came into service, not only single-deckers but double-deckers of the same general pattern, again with central entrance and the streamlined effect.

Strangest of all, perhaps, were the 'boats'. These looked like the single-deckers except that they stopped short at the waist line. They were the modern equivalent of the old open 'toastracks' that had been used for the circular tours around the town. Other cars which gave passengers a chance to sample the sea air were a few open-top double-deck streamliners, but these later acquired roofs.

At the same time as these new trams were being introduced, improvements were being made to the lines on which they were to work. To help speed up the reversal at termini during busy times, turning circles were installed at Starr Gate, Pleasure Beach and Little Bispham.

After the war further new rolling stock was obtained. Experiments led to the introduction in 1952 of the 'Coronations', central-entrance streamliners like the pre-war versions but of more striking design and with more modern equipment.

These cars are the longest in the fleet, being 50 feet in length. In addition they are wider, the relaying of the tracks over the years having made it possible to accommodate a width of almost 8 feet, so allowing a more comfortable vehicle. A total of 56 passengers can be carried on transverse seats.

Resilient wheels reduce running noise, while 'Vambac' electrical equipment provides smooth acceleration and four motors permit a maximum speed of 40 or 45 miles an hour. The entrance has sliding doors, while there are curved windows at roof level to let in the maximum light and to allow passengers a wide angle of vision which is particularly appreciated when viewing the set-pieces of the illuminations. Twenty-five of this class, numbered 304 to 328, were eventually placed in service on the promenade.

In 1960 came the first of the ten new trailers, numbered T1 to T10. Experiments had been made in 1958 with a motor car rebuilt as a trailer and hauled behind an ordinary single-decker. Experience with this led to the new vehicles to work behind modified pre-war cars.

The trailers seat 66 passengers and are some 44 feet long. In appearance they are similar to the familiar single-deck streamliners, but as they have to be hauled by ordinary cars, special attention was paid in their design and construction to making them as light in weight as possible. The two coupled together are over 80 feet in length, an impressive sight that gives Blackpool promenade almost the look of a modern Continental tramway.

III

One Horse Power
(Douglas)

U NLESS you know what to expect you are likely to be surprised when you get off the boat at Douglas. Although the horse trams appear in the advertisements as one of the attractions of the Isle of Man, it is still incredible to find that they really exist. Yet there they are clip-clopping along the promenade.

Once there were more than 14,000 trams running in Britain, on great electrified networks throughout the country. What rash prophet would have dared to foretell that one day a small tramway which had missed the advance of electrification would be among the last survivors? But now the impossible has happened, and you can put the transport clock back 80 years by setting foot on this little island in the Irish Sea.

It was as long ago as 1876 that horse trams began running at Douglas. At first it was only a single track with a mere three cars, but by 1890 the line had reached the end of the promenade at Derby Castle, while by 1897 it had been extended to Victoria Pier. By this time the track had been doubled and the fleet had grown to more than 30.

The first owners were the Douglas Bay Tramway Company, but in 1902 the undertaking was acquired by Douglas Corporation who have owned it ever since. Under municipal guidance it continued to flourish at a time when the Isle of Man was at the peak of its popularity as a pre-eminent holiday resort for the industrial populations of the north of England. By the outbreak of the First World War no fewer than 45 cars were in stock.

Somehow electrification never occurred. Perhaps they did not like the idea of having overhead wires on the sea front, perhaps the seasonal nature of the traffic was not considered to justify it, or perhaps they were just lovers of animals.

On the other hand they may have realised that as the horse-drawn tramways of the mainland were disappearing fast before the new motive power there would be novelty value in such a mode of transport. Moreover, this value would increase as the years went by, and the line would become one of the attractions of the place, a factor that the experienced holiday caterers of Douglas were not slow to appreciate.

So it has come about that the horses have held dominion here ever since. Except for the years of the Second World War the trams have continued to run every summer from May to September, when some 30 of them give a service every few minutes.

The cars themselves can be changed according to the weather. On fine days there are open cross-bench cars, some even without roofs, in which passengers can enjoy the sunshine and savour the ozone. If the weather is not so good a quick-change act brings out the closed saloons.

Although there were formerly some examples of double-deckers of the kind used on urban lines when this form of transport held sway, the whole fleet nowadays consists of single-deckers. The double-deckers are too heavy for one animal in these humane days so they have gone and the one-horse single-deckers have been the rule for a number of years now.

Indeed the work is made as easy as possible for the horses. The cars, for example, run on roller bearings to ensure that they are as free moving as they can be; how far this object has been attained can be judged when you see them being manhandled at the depot. And, of course, the friction of smooth wheels on smooth rails makes it easier to shift a load on rails than on an ordinary road surface, so that even the full complement of 30 or 40 passengers on board does not present too much of a strain.

To help their task still further, the horses are shod with rubber on their shoes to get a good grip without slipping, and this is aided by the special asphalt which forms the road surface between the tracks. To couple them to their charges, the horses wear special spring traces to smooth the shock of the initial inertia when starting the car. Moreover the line is level throughout.

The life of the horses is in striking contrast to that of their forefathers of 70 or 80 years ago. In the days when horse-power ruled the streets, the animals' lot was a hard one. Then they had to be at work in all weathers throughout the year, slipping on the icy surfaces in winter and struggling with an overloaded car or dragging their burdens up steep hills that drastically shortened their lives.

Now schedules are drawn up under the watchful eye of the Royal Society for the Prevention of Cruelty to Animals, although this organisation can find little cause for complaint here. Each horse at Douglas works no more than the four months of the year that the service operates. For the rest of the time he goes into the luxury of winter quarters, to ponder on the past season and await the sunny days again.

No longer are the horses mere drudges. Each is indeed almost a celebrity; he has his own stall in the stable, with his name on it as though it were the dressing room of a stage star. And no little attention is forthcoming from the passengers themselves; nothing is spared for the animals' creature comforts, for when some admirer noticed that they were inconvenienced by the dazzling sun on a hot day they were bedecked with gay sun bonnets.

When fresh horses are required they are imported from Ireland, but before they can be put to work they have to be broken in. First of all they are taken for a walk along the line to familiarise them with the terrain. They have to learn how to start and stop a car without jerking, and to stand still at stops. They also have to become accustomed to the other traffic they will meet on the promenade, as well as their human cargoes. During this training period the newcomers can be seen being put through their paces before entering active service.

Looking after the animals calls for some unusual jobs not to be found on other transport undertakings. There is the blacksmith who has the task of seeing that his charges are properly shod. And there is the veterinary surgeon who ministers to the health of the animals – once upon a time, sickness among the horses could cause the whole of a town's public transport to come to a halt.

And what other transport department nowadays could add to its bill such items as these, which Douglas needs to keep its animals fed for the year: 2,000 sacks of oats, 185 tons of hay, 68 tons of straw, and 14 tons of bran.

As the lights go out and the holidaymakers embark on the last steamers, the cars go back into the depot for another year. There they are overhauled, repainted and polished in readiness for the next season.

To mark the opening each year a ceremony takes place at which a celebrity cuts the tape and takes the reins as the first tram moves off. Recent appropriate choices for this pleasant ceremony have included horsewoman Pat Smythe one year, and another year J. W. Fowler, then chairman of that band of tram-lovers the Light Railway Transport League. Such proceedings help to get the service off to a blaze of publicity.

In 1963 the trams were even patronised by royalty, when Queen Elizabeth the Queen Mother took a ride on No. 44 pulled by horse 'Winston' during her visit to the Isle of Man.

Take a ride on the cars and you can enjoy the quiet and pleasant run. It is a soothing experience; indeed its therapeutic value is well known, and many a crying infant has been soothed to slumber by the gentle motion.

The two-mile journey takes about 15 minutes. This an overall average speed of 8 miles an hour; almost as fast as powerful modern diesel buses can now make their way through the heart of London or Glasgow at busy times, a wry comment on progress over 80 years!

Being alive (in the literal rather than the electrical sense) the motive power can bring some problems that are not encountered with other forms of traction. Once, a parrot in one of the houses along the route learned to imitate the sound of the car bells so faithfully that it could sabotage everything by bringing the horses to a standstill when they heard the sound.

At another time a horse suddenly 'went on strike' while on duty, refused to go on, and finally had to be led away, leaving one of his fellows to draw the forsaken car back to the depot. But such minor contretemps are rare, and normally the system functions quite happily and is a continuing attraction to visitors.

Is it the last horse tramway in the world? Even now it would be a bold

assertion to answer yes. Strange rumours persist about lines in the wilds of
Mexico, and intrepid travellers have brought back tales of weird animal-
powered vehicles than run on tracks from station to farm and are parked
outside the front door just as though they were the family's private motor
car.

Even within the United Kingdom until 1957 it was possible to ride on
a horse tram at Fintona in Ireland, where such a vehicle functioned on a
railway branch line. And for one brief period in 1963 the Tramway Museum
Society operated a horse tram at their Crich museum, but this has now given
way to electric traction. Nowadays it is certain that you would have to go a
long way to find another Douglas, although America's Disneyland offers a
similar attraction.

The horse cars are not the only trams to have operated in Douglas. There
was once also a cable-worked line that followed a U-shaped course, starting
from the promenade at each end and wandering through the streets of the
town. This functioned from 1896 to 1929.

Farther along the coast, to the southward, there were electric trams
on the Marine Drive from Douglas to Port Soderick. This was a precipitous
road clinging to the cliffs and providing a pleasant ride for holidaymakers.

This service ended with the war in 1939, although the cars remained
in situ, marooned in their cliff-top depot for many more years simply because
of the difficulty of removing them. The last traces have now been obliterated
by the building of the new Marine Drive. The cars were double-deckers,
with open tops and open sides on the lower deck, and the line had the distinction of being the only one on the island of standard 4 ft. 8½ in. gauge, most
of the others past and present having been of 3 ft. gauge.

At the Derby Castle terminus the horse cars meet another rail survivor,
for this is also the terminus of the Manx Electric Railway. The MER, though,
is quite different from the Douglas undertaking; the cars might look just as
'period' but this time they are electrically driven. They are long single-
deckers, many of them dating back to the earliest days of the line which
opened in 1899. Most are of the saloon type, with the entrances sited on the
corners at the end, while others are of the cross-bench type, with open sides
to allow passengers to enjoy the scenery and sea breezes.

For the MER route is a scenic one, some 17 miles long from Douglas
to Laxey and Ramsey. It is double track and on its own right of way as
it passes glens and woods with glimpses of the sea. From Laxey, about the
mid point of its course, another electric line climbs up to the top of Snaefell;
this mountain railway uses a central 'third rail' which is gripped by wheels
on the car to serve as an effective brake on the steep gradients.

IV

Trams in a Quarry
(Crich Museum)

WHO would suspect that the bleak Derbyshire hills conceal a hideout for fugitive trams? Drive from the spa town of Matlock or approach from the plain of Derby, and as the hills loom up in front there is a church tower and a war memorial against the skyline. Beneath it lies a quarry, in which retired trams now have a new lease of life.

'Life' is the operative word here, for this museum is something more than stuffed specimens in glass cases. This is not a static exhibit, it is a real working tramway. On a summer Sunday, crowds come here to take a nostalgic ride on a type of vehicle that to most people is only a memory. The once familiar ring of the gong, the swish of the trolley, the hum of the motors, are kept alive here for those who might otherwise forget the trams that once served so well in Britain's towns.

Come into Crich and have a look at the museum. Drive up through the main street of the village, turn left at the top of the hill, and there is the most incongruous sight imaginable.

Green-painted standards support glistening overhead wires that extend away into the distance. Waiting by the entrance to the museum site is a gleaming red-and-white double-deck tram, surrounded by people taking photographs or about to board for a ride. Soon along the line comes another tram, this time an open-sided single-decker. It negotiates the points and comes to a stand at the terminus alongside the double-decker.

Get on and you are back in the world of 40 years ago. On the lower deck are swingover seats, as well as the longitudinal benches at the end where passengers sat facing each other. The stairs are narrow and steep and curving, and on the top deck are hard polished wooden seats. Judging by the condition of the whole vehicle you would hardly imagine that it had seen many years of service in the streets of its native town before coming to its new home.

The conductor rings the bell and the car starts its journey, enabling you to see the extent of the museum. Leaving the terminus it passes the old stone building from which can be heard the roar of the generator that supplies current to the line. On the right-hand side a stationary tram serves as a bookshop, in which visitors can buy relevant photographs and literature. Soon the car passes the depots where an impressive array of tracks fan out into the sheds.

As you go by there is just time to see a fascinating line-up of trams of all types and colours, and then you jog over the points and continue the journey. By now the line is away from the busiest part of the site and is running in a grass-lined and tree-shaded cutting. The tracks curve into the distance, with the face of the quarry and the memorial rising high up on the right.

All too soon journey's end is reached. The trolley boy leaps out to change the pole round, the driver takes his controller key and goes to the other end in readinesss for the return. Inside there is a sort of 'general post' as everyone gets up and swings the seats round so that they are facing the right way.

A quick check to see that all is in order, the conductor rings the bell and the car is off again. Then comes the clickety-click of the rail joints and the hiss of the trolley until it slows down for the depot points again and negotiates the busy part of the route into the terminus, where another loaded car is ready to make the round trip.

Now take a look into the depots and see something of the wide range of cars here. There are some 40 in all – more than many 'real' tramways had in their heyday!

There is a large green bogie double-decker from Blackpool. This has open balconies and is numbered 40. By coincidence there is another No. 40, also from the same town; this is a Blackpool and Fleetwood Tramroad saloon of 1914.

Then there is Southampton No. 45, an open-top double-decker of a design that was once common on many British systems. This dates from 1903. It has a special significance here, for this was really the one that started the whole business, being the first tram that was preserved by amateurs and thus providing the inspiration for the museum.

Sheffield trams are conspicuous here. There is No. 46, a single-decker of the type that was used in the city for its first electric operation in 1899. In contrast comes No. 189 of 1934, an all-enclosed double-decker, while of even more modern design is No. 510. This is a streamliner built in 1950 and one of the last trams constructed for use in Britain. After a life of only ten years it had the unenviable distinction of being the last to run in Sheffield, and was then taken away for preservation, still with its 'Last Tram' decorations on it.

Glasgow is also well represented. Typical of the earlier generation is No. 22, an open-balcony double-decker of 1922, resplendent in the livery of its youth. By contrast No. 1297 is a mere youngster dating only from 1948 and known as the 'Cunarder'.

The Leeds system is depicted by several generations of rolling stock. There is No. 399 of 1926 and No. 180 of 1931, both of them four-wheel all-enclosed double-deckers of the kind that was found on many undertakings.

Nearby are two of the most modern British trams, also hailing from Leeds. No. 602 is a streamlined single-decker in a glorious purple livery, so finished because it entered service in the Coronation year of 1953, while No. 600 dates from 1954 and is another single-decker. These were experimental

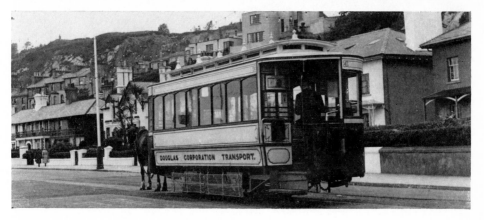

Horse trams on the Promenade at Douglas, Isle of Man. Upper, a passenger's eye view; second, an unusual way of moving a tram is to tow it behind a bus; lower, when the weather is not so good the enclosed cars are brought out.

(*J. H. Price, W. J. Wyse*)

PLATE 3

A busy day at the Crich Tramway Museum. Passengers prepare to board an ex-Blackpool cross-bench car of 1898. *(J. Joyce*

Part of the running line at the Crich museum, showing its location in the quarry. *(J. Joyce*

PLATE 4

Two examples of the large bogie double-deckers that characterised the London tramways. On the right is an ex-West Ham car, while below is an ex-London County Council E/3 Class of the type used on the Kingsway Subway services. Note the 'Via Kingsway Subway' boards on the side, also the location of the plough carrier between the bogies. *(J. Joyce*

PLATE 5

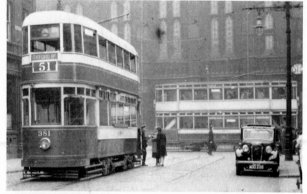

Three types of Manchester tram. Above, the typical bogie double-decker; left, the 'Pilcher'; and below, the single-deck 'California'.

(W. A. Camwell

PLATE 6

vehicles but they had very short working lives, for their home lines ceased operation in 1959.

The fact that these three systems of Glasgow, Sheffield and Leeds have so many representatives at Crich is largely due to the fact that they survived long enough for the museum to be under way to provide a new home for them. But the museum has also been lucky enough to obtain specimens from tramways that ceased at earlier dates.

Gateshead single-decker No. 5, for example, was rescued from its later stamping ground, the Grimsby and Immingham Electric Railway. Then there is Gateshead No. 52, a little single-decker which braved several years in someone's back garden after it had ended its work in 1951. There is also a water car from Cardiff, a double-decker from Hull and another from Leicester.

And not content with combing Britain, the Society has spread its net abroad. It has brought a 90-year-old horse car from Portugal, and – the most ambitious traveller of all – an early electric open-balcony double-decker from Johannesburg in South Africa.

Many of the exhibits when they were obtained were not in the pink of condition after many years of service. When they reached Crich they were often badly in need of maintenance, reconstruction and repainting. Moreover, even when they arrived at the museum, they often had to spend time out in the open until depots could be erected to provide covered storage, and in the damp atmosphere of Derbyshire they were subject to rapid deterioration unless they were well looked after. A great deal of effort has had to be put into maintaining this varied collection.

It is not only the cars themselves that have had to be brought from their far-flung destinations; track and equipment has also had to be obtained. As tramways have gone out of business the museum has acquired items to build up its own new tramway, until a complete working system has been put together, utilising a piece from here and another piece from there.

All this has been achieved entirely by voluntary effort. The creation of the museum has not been the work of a wealthy corporation or a large municipality, but of a small but vigorous band of enthusiasts.

The Tramway Museum Society was formed in 1955, at a time when it was clear that very soon the tram in Britain would almost completely disappear unless steps were taken to preserve some specimens. The Society is a voluntary organisation with unpaid officers and spare-time workers who wanted to see a museum created to mark the standing of this form of transport.

Trams are big things and they require space to keep them in, but it was not until 1959 that a satisfactory site was discovered when the old quarry at Crich became available and was judged suitable for the purpose. Although in some respects it is out of the way, it is in a central position (it is almost in the exact geographical centre of England), land was fairly cheap away from urban areas, and it allowed sufficient room for an operating line to be built.

Then week by week and month by month members of the Society have braved the cold and snow of winter and the sun and dust of summer to come to this desolate place to work towards their object. Most are amateurs to the transport business, so they have had to learn the new job from the beginning.

Work has included levelling land, making foundations, laying track, and putting up overhead standards and wires, as well as erecting depots and maintaining the vehicles. There has also been the task of arranging the transport of cars from all over Britain, a costly and often difficult matter when it is realised that many are double-deckers that are too high to go under some bridges, and that distances may involve several hundred miles from, for example, Glasgow – or even thousands of miles from South Africa. There have also been legal complexities over land and amenities, in addition to efforts in raising money to keep the whole project going.

The Society has had to learn the hard way. It has had to find out how the business of construction and operation are carried on. Members can now appreciate something of the problems of the people who laid the first tramways, but it is now so long since all this happened that it has meant in effect starting from scratch. How, for example, do standards have to be put up and how do wires have to be strung? Then there are the intricacies of the mixed rolling stock; what other operator has had a fleet where every car is different? They are different ages, shapes and sizes, and each has its own peculiarities.

It was naturally a great day in 1963 when the official first run was made over a few yards of track, using an 1874 Sheffield horse car. Behind the inaugural journey was not only all the work, but some trepidation about the actual operation – how would the horse take to it?

Already tales of those days have passed into the folklore of Crich; how two people had to hold the horse, then jump clear as the conductor sounded the bell and the horse bounded forward – the end of the line came almost before most passengers realised they had even started their journey. One day the horse broke loose and trotted briskly away, but then – well-trained animal that he was – he stopped at the 'terminus' and waited patiently until his breathless crew could catch up with him.

Soon, like his predecessors of 60 or 70 years ago, he was to be overtaken by modernisation and the march of progress as electrification went ahead.

Through the winter, members toiled; digging holes for standards, putting up the wires, and trying to solve the problems of a suitable power supply. The local supply was inadequate for the drastic needs of traction motors (indeed who could have foreseen such a need in such a place?) so the museum had to resort to its own supply in the shape of a motor-generator set, which now hums away merrily in its shed when the line is running.

So in 1964 the first electric operation commenced, bringing to fruition the hopes of the Society's creators. But they were not content to rest on their laurels and soon plans were in hand for extending the line away into the distance.

Already the Crich museum has established itself as a tourist attraction, while to the transport enthusiast it is a fascinating spot where he can see trams of the past, not as dead relics but in actual operation, carrying passengers along the rails as they were intended to do. But above all the museum is a tribute to all those who have worked to make a dream a reality.

V

Shilling All Day
(London)

EVEN in their heyday you could have visited London without seeing any trams, for they never penetrated some of the central districts. But if you went to places like the Elephant and Castle, Stratford Broadway, or the Angel at Islington, you soon became aware of the complexity of this vast system with its great double-deckers serving innumerable routes into the endless suburbs.

London's first tramways were three lines built by the American George Francis Train and opened in 1861. They ran along Bayswater Road, along Victoria Street, and from Westminster Bridge to Kennington, as three separate lines with no connection between them. Their lives were short, and they were all gone within about a year.

Many objections were made to this new venture. It was claimed that the rails were dangerous to other traffic. As Train used the 'step' rail which, instead of being level with the rest of the surface, left a ridge along the roadway, there was some justification for this view. Train was also unlucky in his choice of routes for they were in the better-class areas where the carriage folk of Bayswater and Westminster did not take kindly to the public conveyance.

London had to wait several years before it again had trams. Then in 1870 the Metropolitan Street Tramways Company inaugurated its line from Kennington to Brixton, followed a few days later by the North Metropolitan Tramways route from Whitechapel to Bow. After this a network of horse tramways came into existence.

In 1884 mechanical traction was introduced on steep Highgate Hill; this was the first cable tramway in Europe and it continued to operate (although with some interruptions) until 1909. Another cable line, between Kennington and Streatham, was opened later and this ceased in 1905.

But in spite of these efforts mechanical traction on a large scale was introduced relatively late. Although steam locomotives were used by the North London Tramways Company in 1885, the steam tram was not popular in London as it was in the Midlands and North of England.

Apart from an experiment at Alexandra Palace in 1898, electric traction on London's tramways was inaugurated by the London United Tramways in 1901 on routes from Shepherds Bush and Hammersmith to Acton and

Kew. Electrification followed in East Ham and Croydon, and then in 1903 the London County Council began operation of its conduit system of electrification when services started between Westminster, Waterloo, Blackfriars and Tooting.

After this, development was rapid and the trams reached the height of their glory in the 1920s. By this time the tracks extended right across the capital from Waltham Cross in the north to Purley in the south, and from Uxbridge in the west to Dartford in the east.

In 1933 all the tramways in London came under the control of the London Passenger Transport Board, which thus inherited a fleet of 2,629 cars operating over a route mileage of some 328. The fleet came from eleven different operators, both municipal and company; the London County Council contributed 1,663 cars, the Metropolitan Electric Tramways 315, the London United Tramways 150, West Ham Corporation 134, Walthamstow Council 62, East Ham Corporation 56, Croydon Corporation 55, the South Metropolitan Tramways 52, Leyton Council 50, Ilford Corporation 40, Bexley Council 33, and Erith Council 19.

Yet perhaps the beginning of the end was already in sight in 1931, when the London United introduced London's first trolleybus services in replacement of trams in the suburban areas of Teddington and Kingston. Soon after its formation the LPTB drew up plans for further conversions, and this programme went ahead rapidly during the years 1935 to 1940, affecting especially routes in the north, west and east.

The war interrupted the changeover before it could be completed, so that the trams in south London were given a reprieve until post-war conditions made it possible to dispense with them. When the time came, though, they were replaced by motor buses and not by trolleybuses, which were themselves soon to disappear. The last tram ran in 1952.

As might be expected of a network so vast and of such diverse origins, there were many unusual and interesting features.

One of these was the conduit system, which continued right to the end. Similar to that once used in Blackpool, in London it was developed by the LCC to meet the objection to overhead wires which amenity-conscious folk would not permit to disfigure the streets. It was a costly alternative involving the digging of a channel between the rails and the laying of two conductor rails to carry the current. As with the Blackpool conduit, there was a slot in the roadway between the running lines, and the car was fitted with a 'plough' which passed through this slot to make contact with the conductor rails. The London method of construction, however, was much more substantial than that in Blackpool.

In the outer areas where there was less objection to the overhead wires, these were installed and there were change pits where the car shed its plough and put up a trolley pole to take current from the overhead in the normal way.

Although the conduit generally gave good service over a period of nearly half a century, in its later days it suffered from defects such as broken ploughs getting jammed in the slot, while it was always possible for a car to get stuck 'on the dead' at a junction – where there had to be gaps in the conductor rails to allow two lines to cross – and then it had to wait for a push from the one behind. Knowing this latter peculiarity, LCC drivers adopted the technique of taking a run at a junction, in order that momentum would take them over the dead spot, whereas drivers elsewhere would go slow over the points.

At the centre of the London network were two distinctive parts of tramway topography – the Embankment and the Kingsway Subway. The Victoria Embankment is one of London's most impressive highways, arcing in a great curve beside the River Thames for about a mile from Blackfriars to Westminster. Along this stretch the trams ran at one side of the carriageway so that they were virtually on their own right of way, allowing a fast haul for the enormous amount of traffic they carried. At the height of operation some 200 cars an hour passed this way in each direction.

The Kingsway Subway was unique in Britain. Opened in two sections, in 1906 and 1908 respectively, it ran from Theobalds Road in Holborn, under the new thoroughfare of Kingsway – the subway and the street were built at the same time – then under Aldwych to join the Embankment lines, emerging into the open near Waterloo bridge.

At first only single-deckers could use the subway, but in 1930 and 1931 it was enlarged to take double-deckers. When the present Waterloo Bridge was built it resulted in the trams coming out immediately beneath the wide span of the bridge. The subway continued in use until 1952, and now its southern part has been reconstructed as an underpass for motor traffic.

If the Embankment was at the centre of the network, that network itself was of a strange shape. Its main defect was that it had large gaps in the middle, which divided the north from the south. Numerous plans were put forward for joining the gaps – including long subways beneath new streets – but this was never done, and thus many main streets in the West End and the City remained tramless. Gaps, such as those between Blackfriars and Farringdon Street and between Victoria and Paddington, meant that cross-city services by tram were non-existent, except via the Kingsway Subway, and they also meant that buses were always important and competitive.

Cheap fares were another feature of the London tramways. Credit for the introduction of workmen's fares goes to the North Metropolitan company, which in 1871 started a workmen's service from Stratford to Aldgate, so ushering in the era of cheap travel for the masses that the coming of the trams heralded.

The LCC too was notable for its cheap fares, which resulted partly from municipal policy in encouraging people to live out of the most congested areas and in pleasanter surroundings, and partly from motor bus competition. In 1912 maximum fares within the County of London were fixed at 3d.

single and 5d. return, while in 1920 a 2d. midday fare was offered. Passengers were also encouraged to move about their city by such inducements as the '1s. All Day' tickets, by means of which you could travel anywhere within the LCC area for a whole day.

Another unusual aspect of LCC operation was the use of trailer cars. These have always been rare in Britain, but between 1913 and 1924 they were used by the LCC on selected routes in an attempt to deal with the very heavy peak-hour traffic that even exceeded the capability of their large bogie cars. The trailers were open-top double-deck four-wheelers.

In the matter of rolling stock itself a number of types achieved renown. The LCC was well to the fore in employing the covered-top double-decker, introducing in 1907–1908 the E and later the E/1 class, some of which lasted until the final days of operation. One thousand of the E/1 class were purchased by the LCC, probably the largest number of any one type ever built for one operator in this country. The fact that such an order was warranted gives an indication of the size of the Council's fleet and the scale of the traffic it handled.

Among the most famous London trams were the 'Felthams', the first of which were placed in service by the London United Tramways in 1931, followed shortly after by the Metropolitan Electric Tramways. Revolutionary-looking vehicles for their time, they were long bogie double-deckers with rounded ends. Outstanding in their design were the separate cabins for the driver, the front exit and the straight stairs. The large vestibules allowed standing space for about 20 passengers.

One hundred of this type were constructed. They marked a distinct break with tradition and were the forerunners of modern cars that made their appearance in cities such as Glasgow and Liverpool during the 1930s. After being taken out of service in London, the majority of the Felthams had a new lease of life in Leeds where some of them continued at work until operations ceased there also in 1959.

VI

In the Cotton Capital
(Manchester)

MANCHESTER'S first tram ran on *five* wheels. It accomplished this odd feat by having a single central guide wheel which ran in a grooved rail laid between the running rails. The four road wheels had no flanges, their treads simply bearing on the flat outside rails, while the purpose of the fifth wheel was to keep the whole vehicle on the lines.

The point of this ingenious method was that when the tracks came to an end, the guide wheel could be raised and the vehicle could continue its journey along the normal road surface. It was thus something of a hybrid and was as much a bus as anything else. It was a double-decker with seats arranged back-to-back on the roof and with the driver seated at roof level in the usual manner for horse buses.

Known by the grandiloquent name of 'Haworth's Patent Perambulating Principle', it began operation in 1861 on a route to Pendleton in Salford, so it has as much right to be called a Salford vehicle as a Manchester one, even if its claim to be a tram rather than a bus is granted. Although it worked for several years it did not find great favour, and later trams in the area were more conventional vehicles with an even number of wheels.

The first of these orthodox tramways came in 1877, when lines were opened to Bury New Road and Pendleton. Later years saw a whole network come into existence in the streets of the prosperous manufacturing city and its suburbs, spreading not only into the various districts of Manchester itself but transcending municipal boundaries under the aegis of the Manchester Carriage and Tramways Company.

The first section of Manchester's own municipal electric tramways came into operation with due ceremony in 1901 with routes to Cheetham Hill and Hightown. Such was the success of the new mode of traction that in the course of the next two years wires and poles were rapidly erected above the horse lines and the new electrics took over. Progress was so quick that in 1903 the city said goodbye to its horses.

In the years that followed, the electric tram became an accepted part of the streets, conveying an ever-increasing load of humanity. In 1904 over 100 million passengers were carried. By 1914 the number had risen to over 200 million, while in 1924 this had increased to over 300 million.

The tramways reached their peak at the end of the 1920s, when the track

The Glasgow tram in its heyday. This is a 'standard' car before final modernisation to its completely enclosed form. The top deck is painted white; cars were different colours according to the routes they worked.

(A. D. Packer

Below—it was a shock to the unwary to meet a railway engine coming down the street along the tram lines. In Glasgow, shipyards were connected to the railways by way of the tram tracks.

(G. B. Claydon

PLATE 7

Scenes on the Belgian Vicinal tramways. Top, a four-car train at Ostend tram station on the long coastal route. Note the baggage car at the end. Centre, a works car shunting an open-ended trailer. Lower, a four-wheeler used on the Ostend town services.

(J. Joyce)

PLATE 8

An international tram route; a Belgian Vicinal tram ran across the frontier into Holland at Sluis. It is seen here at the customs post.

(W. J. Wyse

A Vicinal 'Autorail' or diesel tram worked a non-electrified route connected with the Belgian coast services at Furnes.

(W. J. Wyse

PLATE 9

A modern Vicinal car of the type used on suburban services in the Brussels area. Behind it are two works cars employed on track reconstruction.
(J. Joyce

Making an interesting contrast in design with the Vicinal car is the PCC of the Brussels city services. Note the bilingual destination indicator, giving place names in both the French and the Flemish forms.
(J. Joyce

PLATE 10

length amounted to over 290 miles, on which there were some 950 cars.

But now the tide was turning. In 1929 it was decided that they should not be extended any further and that no new lines should be built. Costs were high and there was need for new services to suburban housing estates, while the motor bus was considered to be more mobile.

In the following year one of the routes was replaced by buses and this was followed by others, while in 1938 came the first of the trolleybuses. In 1939 the final blow fell when it was decided that the trams should be abandoned altogether. Due to the war the process was necessarily delayed, and it was not until 1949 that the last were withdrawn.

On that foggy January day the last tram was decorated to make the final journey, bringing to a close almost half a century of operation by electric trams, during which time they had carried many millions of passengers and provided cheap and convenient transport. As a reminder of those cheap fares it may be recalled that in 1913 the passenger could travel as far as three miles for as little as 1d.

Manchester's earliest electric trams had open tops and open ends, as was common practice in Britain. But it was soon found that such exposed vehicles were quite unsuited to the Manchester weather, and it was not many years before the top deck was covered in, although the motorman was often left with no windscreen to his platform.

By the 1920s the all-enclosed car was on the scene, and from then on this was typical of the Manchester fleet. A large vehicle, it had seats for some 80 passengers on its two decks.

It ran on maximum-traction bogies, another practice that was common in Britain. On each bogie one motor drove one axle, the other axle merely trailing. The bogie was not pivoted in the centre but towards the motored end, so that most of the weight was carried on the motored axle to provide as much adhesive weight as possible to grip the rails. To enable the car to negotiate sharp curves where the bogie had to swing outwards, the trailing wheels were smaller than the driving wheels so that they could pivot outwards without fouling the frame.

This arrangement gave the best possible performance while avoiding the additional complication, cost and weight of requiring four motors on a bogie car. Since inevitably part of the weight was borne by the unmotored trailing wheels and was not available for adhesion, this type of truck was not suitable for hilly routes where all the weight was needed to get a good grip. However, it was quite satisfactory for a system such as Manchester, where there were few hills to be encountered, and it was also widely adopted in London where similar conditions prevailed.

Inside the car not much attention was paid to comfort. In early days the lower deck was fitted with longitudinal wooden seats on which passengers sat facing each other in two long rows, and it was not until the late 1920s that these were replaced by reversible transverse seats. On the upper deck, wooden seats remained to the bitter end.

Although the bogie double-decker was typical of the fleet, two other types were also to be found. One went under the sunny name of 'California'. This title revealed the origin of the design in the United States, although the Manchester examples were built in Britain and were destined for a climate far removed from that of their namesake.

The California type were single-deckers of a peculiar pattern. In the centre there was a covered-in saloon, but at the ends of this there were long open-sided platforms with seats for passengers who liked the fresh air. Why such a design was adopted for Manchester appears to be something of a mystery, although the need for a single-decker for this particular route was obvious as there were low railway bridges that obviated anything higher.

The Californias were employed only on this one route, the 53 from Cheetham Hill to Brooks Bar. It was a very roundabout way, which was described as 'Circular' although in fact it was not, for the circle was never quite completed. However, it did a pretty good job of boxing the compass, for it wandered almost completely round the city, crossing nearly every other route on the way and putting in an appearance on practically all the main roads until you might have thought that these strange low cars dominated the whole system.

The third Manchester type was the only one that had any pretensions to modernity. It rejoiced in the unofficial but tenacious name of 'Pilcher' after its designer, the then General Manager of the undertaking, Stuart Pilcher, but slight mis-hearing could and did corrupt its name to 'Pilchard'. Officially these were 'Pullmans' to give them some dignity in view of their advanced status and luxurious appointment.

To call the Pilchers 'modern', even by the standards of 1930 when they appeared, is to stretch the term somewhat. Almost their only concessions to modernity were the cushioned seats and curved domed roof. They were indeed an indication of how backward designers of trams were to meet changed conditions. Practically everything in their design was as it might have been some 25 years earlier. This unfortunately applied to others besides these Manchester cars, which admittedly were intended only to wear out the tracks and not to rejuvenate the fleet. But the same point can be made about other towns, where the failure to bring the trams up to date contributed to their unpopularity.

The Pilchers were shorter than their older relatives and were mounted on four wheels instead of on bogies. This was unfortunate, for it meant they lacked the steady riding qualities of the eight-wheelers and soon gained a reputation for bouncing and rocking. This was accentuated in later years as track got into a worse and worse state of disrepair, until a ride in a Pilcher was something to be remembered. Strangely enough, they were sold off when Manchester had finished with them and they eked out the last days of their lives in such widely scattered towns as Sunderland, Leeds, Edinburgh and Aberdeen.

Even on their native ground, though, Manchester's trams were not confined to the streets of their home town. The cotton city itself is surrounded by a ring of towns – Stockport, Oldham, Ashton, Bury, Bolton – all of which had their own municipal systems, which in turn connected with those of Manchester so that the rails extended right across this busy industrial area. Manchester's cars ran on the tracks of several of their neighbours, and it was no surprise to see a red double-decker as far afield as Hazel Grove in Stockport or at Waterhead in Oldham.

Not all this interworking came about without discord. In the early days Manchester and next-door Salford were unable to agree on through-running, with the result that it was possible to see cars turning back when they reached the bridge over the River Irwell, for this was the boundary between the two warring concerns.

However, this state of siege did not last long, and in the years that followed there was a growing intermingling of services between Manchester and nearby towns, so that the differing liveries splashed their own touches of colour in the streets. Through-running arrangements were reached with both Oldham and Ashton as early as 1907, while similar agreements were made with Stockport in 1922 and with Rochdale in 1925.

The extent of the whole network can be judged by the fact that to Manchester's fleet of 950 had to be added some 230 of Salford, 90 of Rochdale, 150 of Oldham, 160 of Bolton, 60 of Bury, 80 of Stockport, and 60 of the grandly-named Stalybridge, Hyde, Mossley and Dukinfield Joint Board.

In Manchester itself, the constant procession of trams imparted bustle to the dignity of the streets. The city is blessed with wide thoroughfares, and along many of these the double tracks formed an impressive centrepiece. In broad Piccadilly there was even room for three tracks abreast where cars could pass or reverse while others loaded and unloaded. Elsewhere complicated one-way layouts sent trams disappearing down one street and reappearing from another.

In the suburbs there were a few examples of reserved tracks where the rails were laid on sleepers on their own strip of land in the centre of a dual carriageway. Most impressive of these was the line along Kingsway, which was opened in 1926. Here were over two miles of reserved track on the route to East Didsbury in the southern suburbs. Not far from this there was another section of sleeper track, over a mile in length, along Princess Road to the lugubriously-named destination of 'Southern Cemetery'.

Other odd destinations were also to be found in the area. Who would want to go to 'Fog Lane'? Perhaps more attractive in name was 'Irlams o' the Height'.

So large a system could be expected to have its own characteristics, and something of this was seen in the cars themselves; in one way at least the livery was the very opposite of the usual. Normal practice was to have the rocker panel (which formed the lower part of the bodywork just above the wheels) painted white or cream, while the upper part above the waistline was painted the fleet colour.

In Manchester, however, it was just the other way round; the rocker panel was red while the upper panel was cream. Thus even with the cars of so many different operators mingling in the streets the Manchester vehicles could be clearly distinguished at a glance.

Another unusual practice was the employment of 'trolley boys'. Their duty was to see that the trolley pole stayed on the wire when it should – sometimes it needed careful guiding over complicated junctions – and to turn it at the terminus. They also had to help the conductor in his duties. Trolley boys were first used in 1902 and they lasted as late as 1933. They meant that each car had the extravagance of a crew of three, something that could only be tolerated in an era of cheap labour, and a sure sign that this was a profitable mode of transport.

A further peculiarity was that the conductor was never called a conductor, as he generally was elsewhere. Manchester did not have any personages so undignified as conductors; they had 'guards'.

An odd tramway in the area was that to Trafford Park, which for a time used gas-powered trams. The service ran for several years to convey workers to the industrial districts of Trafford Park. It was in part superseded by electric cars, but the gas trams continued to function until 1908.

VII

On the Banks of the Clyde
(Glasgow)

'TWENTY-TWO miles for 2d.' should be enough to attract the most hardened bargain hunter, to say nothing of the thrifty Scot. That is what the Glasgow trams offered, and if they are remembered for no other reason they will be remembered for such absurdly low fares. This was an example dating from the 1920s when bus competition was being felt; for this small amount the traveller could go all the way from Airdrie to Paisley or from Renfrew to Milngavie.

The only drawback was that nobody – except perhaps the keen enthusiast – wanted to make such a journey. A glance at a map will show why, for all these destinations were at the outer extremities of the network, and the journeys involved travelled from one side of the built-up area to another, often by a long, slow and roundabout way. Nevertheless these cut prices offered excellent publicity.

Moreover, they were not so out of line with the rest of the fares, for the Glasgow trams were always noted for cheap travel. For many years ½d. adult fares were available.

The importance of the tramways in providing cheap transport can hardly be overemphasised. They were a potent factor in enabling the city to expand and in making it possible for people to live in pleasanter suburbs on the edge of town.

Scotland's largest city, Glasgow is situated on the banks of the River Clyde and now has a population of well over one million. The Clyde, of course, is world famous for its ships, and shipbuilding has long been one of the major industries of Glasgow; a ride on the tram to Clydebank or Renfrew took the passenger past the towering cranes and the giant hulls of ocean liners under construction. Connected with this were industries such as engineering and steelmaking, as well as the busy quays and warehouses of a major port. All told, it was an area where mass transport could find a ready market.

Glasgow's first tramway came into operation in 1872, when a two-mile line started along Great Western Road between St. George's Cross and Eglinton Toll. The owner was a man named Menzies, who treated his customers to a high standard of comfort, for the cars had red plush seats and were adorned with colourful tartan designs. The venture was a success and by 1874 the Glasgow Tramway and Omnibus Company possessed over 100 trams.

Other lines were built and in the 1880s the fleet had risen to over 200. By the early 1890s some 50 million passengers were being carried every year.

While in the early days British tramways were often owned and operated by a company, provision was made for compulsory purchase by the municipality in which the lines ran. Such general power was given by the Tramways Act of 1870, under which the municipality had the power of purchase after 21 years. When that time approached in Glasgow the Corporation decided to exercise its option.

Unfortunately the Corporation and the company found it impossible to come to terms. The result was that the company went out of the business, leaving the Corporation with the task of filling the gap. In a very short space of time it had the tremendous job of conjuring up a whole fleet, a stud of horses and an operating staff, as well as depots and an organisation to begin the running of its own transport undertaking. Somehow it managed the impossible, and in 1894 the first of the Corporation's own trams started.

Soon a new factor was to enter the scene, for by this time the power of electricity was in evidence. It was clear that the days of animal traction were numbered, and plans were made for electrification. In 1898 the first electric route was opened between Mitchell Street and Springburn.

Two types of car were introduced for the new era. One was an open-top double-decker, the other a bogie single-decker. This latter type was a long centre-entrance vehicle with two saloons, one of which was for smokers and had no glass in the windows. It did not prove popular and the double-decker was to reign supreme in future years.

Electrification progressed rapidly and was completed in 1901, by which time the Corporation had well over 300 cars. In the few years since it had taken over, the number of passengers carried had risen from 54 million to some 140 million a year.

Extensions went ahead steadily, with new lines reaching out into growing suburbs, and the trams became not only a recognised part of the street scene but an object of civic pride. They provided rapid and cheap services for the working man, and they contributed useful sums of money to the municipal exchequer. By 1914 the fleet numbered about 850.

The inter-war years saw further expansion so that by 1933 the stock had reached well over 1,000. In spite of bus competition the cars held their own. Even during the 1930s there were extensions, including to Milngavie in 1934 and to Bellahouston Park for the Empire Exhibition in 1938. The Exhibition also brought forth brilliant newcomers, the famous 'Coronations', the first of which appeared in 1936 and 1937; soon 150 of them were to be in service to revive this mode of transport.

Even after the war there were still signs of vigour, for two further extensions were opened in 1949 while another 100 modified Coronations were put into service between 1948 and 1952. By this time, though, the future of the trams was very much in the balance.

Several factors helped to swing the scales against them. The enormously increased number of vehicles coming on to the roads added to congestion. Glasgow's streets are not as wide as they might be, and in the central area there was no room to provide separate right of way or even loading islands.

Then there was the need to serving housing estates growing up on the outskirts of the city as slums were cleared; the cost of extending the tracks was found to be too high to be practicable and those services were therefore undertaken by buses.

There was also the problem of obtaining new rolling stock. Much of the fleet was in urgent need of replacement, but costs were rocketing sky-high. After some services had given way to buses and trolleybuses, it was at last decided that the whole of the tramways should be abandoned, with the result that the last of them ran in 1962.

With their end came the end of what had seemed a characteristic part of the city. Not least in the essence of this was the typical tram; not the modern Coronation but the old standard car.

The 'standards' were quite unbelievable. In their later years, when you were used to the era of streamlining and jet planes, they looked extremely antiquated with their profusion of angles and polished wood. In appearance they seemed top-heavy and you expected them to topple over as they swayed around the curves.

The lower deck windows had decorative rounded tops, while the upper deck was wider than the lower, which was made even worse by sloping inwards to the wheels. The whole was capped by a flat roof. The end view was even more alarming, for the driver's windows came down low so as to give him a good view of the road ahead (although seemingly little protection) while the headlamp was mounted almost at the base of the dash only just above the bumper, imparting a somewhat woebegone expression.

The 'standards' had started life in a much more elemental form. They originated in a fleet of several hundred ordered for the electrification between 1900 and 1902, although others appeared in later years. In their early days they had open platforms and open top decks, a popular arrangement at that period.

Later on the top deck was enclosed, although the ends were still left open. Then in the years from 1928 to 1935 they were 'modernised' when they had the ends of both decks enclosed. They were also re-equipped to bring them up to more modern levels, with new trucks containing motors of higher speed and higher power (60 horse power each as against only 30) so that their performance was more in keeping with the motor traffic with which they now had to share the roads.

For safer and quicker stopping from the high speeds, they were given air-operated brakes to supplement the handbrake on which they had previously relied. The comfort of passengers was catered for by the installation of upholstered seats in place of the wooden ones.

The end product had some affinity with the Irishman's knife, which had had six new blades and half a dozen new handles but was still essentially the same implement. Some of the cars battled on for 50 or 60 years, lively to the last. This was much longer than they should have lasted, but the war slowed down the projected renovation programme which should have seen their replacement.

Their existence was always something of an embarrassment whenever the future of the system was under discussion, and they helped to weigh the balance against the trams as their cost of replacement by this time was too great. However, there is no doubt that the canny Glaswegians had their money's worth out of them.

By contrast it is interesting to compare the 'standards' with the Coronations. These were bogie cars with four 35-horse-power motors and with contactor control for smooth and rapid acceleration. They were 34½ feet long and weighed over 20 tons. The streamlined bodies with upholstered seats for 65 passengers had long open saloons unencumbered by internal bulkheads, while there were doors to the platforms. The degree of comfort and performance was far superior to the old-timers, and also – many thought – to the contemporary bus.

Longevity among the rolling stock was one feature of the tramways. Coupled with it, of course, was the longevity of the system itself, for Glasgow still had its trams long after other British cities had scrapped theirs. Thus it was something of a shock for the unwary visitor to go to Glasgow and see the main streets lined with tracks and long processions of trams; it was like putting the clock back some 30 years to the time when such a sight was commonplace. Many felt that such a form of transport was outmoded, and controversy raged about its future, some people insisting that it was high time that Glasgow brought itself into line with other places.

Another aspect of the system was its great size. Even after the Second World War there were still some 1,000 trams. This was one reason why the conversion took so long, for apart from anything else the task of replacement was a physical one of some magnitude.

Large assets in the shape of equipment and a power station were tied up, while the fleet with its track and overhead represented a considerable asset which could not be lightly thrown away. And even with the most indecent haste it was not easy, especially in the post-war era of shortages, to sweep the trams away too rapidly. Even so the majority went in a period of about five years.

The cars ran not only in Glasgow itself but went far beyond the boundaries. In Britain it had been rare for a municipal operator to run tramways beyond its boundaries, but in Glasgow they extended far afield. During the expansionary period the lines were laid to outlying suburbs, sometimes arousing indignation in that such facilities were provided for folk who were not

Representing current German tramway practice is this three-section articulated car in Stuttgart.

(Courtesy 'Über Berg und Tal')

PCC-cars in The Hague. These are the earlier versions with small windows in characteristic American style. *(W. J. Wyse*

A London tram of East Ham origin, negotiating the roundabout at Eltham shortly before abandonment. The 'Last Tram Week' notice can be seen on the side of the car. *(W. J. Wyse*

Type V6 motor tram and trailer in Hamburg, running on reserved track at Sievekingsdamm. *(W. J. Wyse*

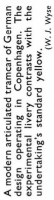

A modern articulated tramcar of German design operating in Copenhagen. The experimental livery contrasts with the undertaking's standard yellow.

(W. J. Wyse

The 'Hovertram', one of Blackpool's striking illuminated trams, emerges from the depot for its journey along the Promenade amid the Illuminations.

(W. J. Wyse)

Glaswegians but who enjoyed the benefit of amenities paid for by the city.

The Corporation also took over other undertakings, when it acquired the formerly independent tramways of neighbouring Airdrie and Coatbridge in 1921 and Paisley in 1923.

This meant that the Corporation's cars penetrated to these towns, in one case a new line on reserved track being laid to connect the formerly isolated Airdrie route to give a fast interurban link between the communities. At one time the situation was such that almost half of the mileage of track covered by the Corporation was 'outwith' the city boundaries.

Two other features were worthy of note. One was the use of colours to indicate routes. Different colours were given to the side panels on the upper decks; thus there were white, blue, red, green and yellow cars, each variety working on different routes so that it was easy to pick out the one you wanted from a row of them in the street.

As far as possible things were so ordered that the same colours were not seen along the same streets. The disadvantage was that if a car was transferred from one route to another it could cause untold confusion, and it was therefore more or less routebound. The colours were eventually given up in favour of the more conventional numbers in the years before the war.

Another peculiarity was the gauge of the track. This was 4 ft. 7¾ in., as against the standard 4 ft. 8½in. which was usual on tramways as well as railways.

The slight difference in the Glasgow gauge was to allow for the running of railway wagons along the tram lines. Although the gauge is the same, it is not possible to run railway wagons on standard-gauge tram lines because the larger flanges and treads of the railway wheels will not fit into the groove. So to allow for this the tram gauge had to be cut down to 4 ft. 7¾ in. to permit the wagons to run on their flanges in the groove of the rails.

This was necessary because railway wagons were conveyed along the tram tracks to and from the shipyards in the Govan area. Many a stranger has gazed in wonder at seeing a steam or electric locomotive hauling wagons along the street, and this practice went on even after the normal passenger service had ended.

Although the trams have now gone, Glasgow Corporation still engages in electric rail operation in the shape of the Subway. This is an underground railway which describes a circle beneath the central districts of the city. There are 15 stations on the 6½-mile circle, and the service is worked by two-car trains, the original stock of 1896-97 still being used. The Subway was formerly cable operated and worked by a separate company, but it was later taken over by the Corporation and was electrified in 1935.

This is not the only electric rail transport in the Glasgow area, for in the last few years British Railways have electrified certain of the suburban railways, with the result that the 'Blue Trains' go as far afield as Airdrie and Balloch. It is interesting to recall that these places were at extremities of the former tram network, so that electric traction has returned over this route, albeit off rather than on the roads.

Some of the railways concerned in the scheme were almost moribund, having been seriously hit by tram and bus competition. Their electrification is now affecting the pattern of transport in the area by taking traffic away from the roads and putting it on to the railways. Under such changing conditions the future of the trams would have been problematical.

VIII

Coastal Marathon
(Belgian Vicinal)

THE English visitor to Belgium is not quite sure what to make of the Vicinal. Is it a tramway or a railway? When you see rails in the streets of Ostend you think it must be a tramway. But what trams! Not like the square double-deckers you remember in Britain, but smart steamliners; and they are not lone vehicles but are coupled into whole trains.

What is more, they soon forsake the streets altogether, and go dashing off across the sand dunes on their own tracks, looking for all the world like a real railway. To confound the matter still further, you find that, although they have conductors, you must take your ticket at a booking office just as though you were making a railway journey.

Until a few years ago things were simpler, for there were little town trams in Ostend to make the mental transition easier. One of the first things you would see as the steamer from Dover came into the harbour was a dainty cream-coloured tram rounding the corner by the quayside and the fishing boats and passing the cafés on the front.

This was a typical Vicinal small-town car, a four-wheeler of the kind used in places such as Bruges, Mechelen and Namur, where they would trundle back and forth along strictly-timetabled single tracks. A fleet of them once served Ostend, making tortuous turns around the narrow streets and pursuing circular routes that could easily confuse the visitor. In Ostend's golden days there were also open-sided cross-bench trailers that went to the town's famous race course. Now these local services have been replaced by red buses.

What remain are the interurbans, the long sleek trains rumbling through the town, but what you see in the town is a mere fraction of the whole. One tram route to end all tram routes and probably the longest in the world, it is some 40 miles long and runs almost the entire length of the Belgian coast. Britain has never had anything quite like this, so the Vicinal can hardly fail to impress.

Having landed from the steamer, you pass through the Customs and the adjoining Quay Station and immediately outside you are confronted by a large notice indicating (in English) 'Tram Station.' Here, with perhaps an interurban train drawing in, is the first glimpse of the Vicinal. The 'station' has a three-track layout with slightly raised platforms, and a neat building which houses the booking office and waiting room. There are also sidings for accommodating spare rolling stock.

The trains generally consist of at least a motor car hauling one trailer. Sometimes there are two or more trailers, while for certain journeys a four-wheel baggage van is added.

The pride of the line are the 'SO' class motor cars, which were introduced in 1955 and 1956. They are smart, fast, smooth-running and comfortable. They have two-and-one seating for 42 passengers as well as room for another 22 standing, and are single-ended for the whole train is turned at each terminus. The entrance is at the rear and the exit at the front, both being provided with power-operated folding doors. There is also a door in the back end to enable the conductor to pass through on to the trailer.

These cars are finished in a cream livery, with a decorative 'moustache' on the front. They were built by the undertaking in its own workshops in Brussels, and although the gauge of the line is only one metre, they are over 7 ft. 6 in. wide, with adequate space for comfortable seating as well as a central gangway.

By comparison the older vehicles they replaced were less exciting, although they were no less solid and respectable. Dating from 1930, they seated 40 passengers in a saloon divided by an internal bulkhead, while there was standing room on the platforms for another 48. On each platform there was a trilingual notice, the English version of which rather quaintly requested 'Please do not distract the Wattman'.

Some of these motors were rebuilt as trailers to go with the new 'SO' class. Until this time there was another generation of older four-wheelers, the trailers of this vintage mostly having open platforms which afforded a splendid observation point for a tour of the line. At times it was not uncommon to see a mixture of types, with a modern motor hauling several four-wheel trailers including one or more of the open-enders.

The stock is maintained in excellent condition – major maintenance being done in the winter months when traffic is lightest – and the result is a service renowned for regularity and punctuality. Here is how one observer could regulate his day by this means:

'One goes to bathe as soon as the 11 o'clock car is heard, and then two trams afterwards it is time for the aperitif.'

The coast route extends some 40 miles from De Panne, near the French frontier, to Knokke-Zoute, near the Dutch frontier. It is double track throughout, and except for several sections of street-running through towns and villages, it is entirely on its own right of way. Sometimes it is at the side of the road, sometimes in the centre of a dual carriageway, and sometimes away from the road altogether.

Stops are limited and may be a mile or more apart. Each is marked by a neat station with a booking office, at which you should obtain your ticket before boarding – if you do not you have to pay an extra 5 francs (about 9d.). This surcharge is imposed by Royal decree, and is to ensure that the fare is paid, for at busy periods the conductor hardly has time to collect all the fares between stops. There are also a number of request stops, which of course do not have any booking office or have it open only at certain times. Good value for the traveller is a one-day ticket at about 11s., or a five-day ticket which is an even better bargain.

This is the Belgian holiday coast and scenically the route presents a string of seaside resorts, hotels, villas, golf courses and camping sites. Through all these the tram is a well-known part of the scene. Here is how one writer described it:

'The tram is an integral part of the environment of our seaside towns. It is not the sea breeze nor the smell of seaweed which is the first impression of the traveller leaving the station; not until he hears the modulated note of the klaxon and sees the familiar tram appear is he sure that he is at the seaside, and only then his holidays begin.'

The route can be considered as two, divided almost equally by Ostend in the middle. Service 1 runs between Ostend and Knokke-Zoute, a distance of nearly 21 miles. The time for the journey is just over an hour, giving a very high average speed of about 19 miles an hour. Service 2 runs between Ostend and De Panne, a distance of just over 20 miles, and again the journey time is a few minutes over the hour, again giving a high average speed of over 17 miles an hour. When it is considered that these speeds compare with the 9 or 10 miles an hour that was typical of the conventional British street tramways, it can be seen that the Vicinal is something out of the ordinary.

Certain journeys are worked right through between De Panne and Knokke or Zoute, and perhaps the most exciting are in summer when 'extras' marked 'De Panne Direct' appear and rush along the tracks at express speed. In winter the service is only hourly, but in summer the traffic increases in intensity until there are three or four trains in an hour.

There are substantial variations in the service, though, and a timetable (or even a calendar) is essential. In fact you are well advised to treat the line as a railway and look up the time of the next train rather than wait at the stop as you would for an ordinary town tram that runs every few minutes.

Leaving Ostend the route to De Panne traverses the streets of the town to reach the sea front at Mariakerke, where it goes on to a reservation at the side of the road along the promenade as far as Middelkerke. This section resembles Blackpool promenade, and is indeed the only part of the whole line that is actually laid along the sea front, although so much of it is situated near the sea. After this there begins a central reservation which continues to Westende Bad, where the route leaves the road and turns inland on private right-of-way through fields to enter the main street of the village of Lombardsijde.

After a section of roadside reservation, Nieuwpoort is reached by a bridge. The route now heads towards the sea again, continuing at the side of the road through Nieuwpoort-an-Zee to Oostduinkerke Bad. From here it is on a central reservation between dual carriageways, although there are sections of street track through Koksijde and St. Idesbald. Reaching De Panne, the route follows the streets of the town to the terminus, where the train disappears round sand dunes to negotiate its turning circle. In earlier days another route ran out of Ostend following a course further inland, to reach Nieuwpoort town and then going on to Furnes.

Back at Ostend again, you find that route 1 to Knokke leaves Ostend by means of bridges over the railway and the harbour. Reservation is soon reached, and then speed increases as the tram continues past the dunes to Bredene-an-Zee. Beyond, the line runs for some distance out of sight of the road and between trees, and this is probably the section where the highest speeds are attained.

The main road is rejoined after Wenduine and is followed to Blankenberge, one of the largest and most popular of the resorts, through which the trams run along the streets. Leaving Blankenberge the line enters a central reservation which, apart from a length over an opening bridge at Zeebrugge, extends through Heyst and on almost to Knokke. Except in the busy months of July and August, it goes on through the streets of the town to the select resort of Le Zoute, but during these two months it terminates rather inconveniently by Knokke railway station. Beyond Le Zoute there used to be a local service through to the Dutch frontier at Siska.

At Knokke there was until 1956 another route which ran inland some 13 miles to the ancient city of Bruges. This was of single track, laid mostly at the side of a country road but with sections in the village streets of Westkapelle and Dudzele. The service was generally provided by single units, which rushed past the fields and farmhouses and paused only at isolated passing loops when the signals showed that another car was due. At Bruges the line encountered the local routes.

Until 1951 yet another line branched off from Westkapelle across into Holland to reach Sluis, while beyond here there used to be steam trams to Breskens. On this international service tram passengers had the unusual experience of customs examinations, and strange tales are told of certain types of intoxicating liquor being smuggled across in the capacious equipment compartments of the car.

Belgium at one time had a nation-wide network of these light railways and tramways operated by the Vicinal – the Société Nationale des Chemins de Fer Vicinaux (SNCV), or in the Flemish version the NatialeMaatschappij voor Buurtspoorwegen (NMVB).

The SNCV was set up in 1884, with capital in part from the state and in part from local authorities. Its object was to sponsor local rail transport in areas which had been neglected by the main lines.

At first it did not undertake the operation of lines itself, but instead leased them out to private companies or local authorities. In later years, though, it did in fact find itself obliged to take over the actual working in many cases. The coastal network was until recently the last main concessionaire and was under the control of the Société pour Exploitation des Lignes Vicinales d'Ostende et des Plages Belges.

In general the Vicinal lines, most of which were of the metre gauge, ran in the streets of towns but were laid as roadside light railways in between. Many of the routes were of single track. Steam traction was the first motive power, and in places this lingered on even into post-war years in spite of the fact that electrification of the principal routes began as early as the 1890s.

On some lines, where traffic was not heavy enough to justify the cost of electrification, diesel railcars or 'autorails' were employed, and sometimes freight was also carried. As well as the interurbans the Vicinal provided local services in towns such as Ostend, Bruges, Namur and Mechelen, in addition to some services in the larger towns.

With the development of the motor bus and the lorry and the widespread use of private cars, the lightly-used lines lost most of their traffic. Many succumbed, although a number continue in operation around Brussels, Antwerp and Charleroi, while the coastal route remains the showpiece.

IX

Mixed-Gauge and Subway
(Brussels)

A N Englishman started the first tramway in Brussels. That was in 1869 when William Morris brought this new mode of transport to the Belgian capital by importing trams from his homeland. Like those he knew at home they were double-deckers, but unlike the British the Belgians did not take readily to the open top deck, and so for many years now Brussels has had the inevitable Continental-type single-deckers.

However, after this start, the tramways in the city went on growing, with at one time a number of different companies which were later amalgamated. During the early period another odd form of vehicle was used; this was a five-wheeler, not unlike the 'patent perambulating vehicle' of Salford, for it consisted of a bus with a fifth wheel which fitted into the rails.

Electrification of the horse-car lines began in 1894, and soon the overhead wires were to be seen over a wide area of the city and its suburbs.

Not everywhere, though. For in the centre of the historic city, there was – as there was at this time in many towns – a fear that the jungle of poles and wires would disfigure the splendid streets. In certain thoroughfares, therefore, the installation of overhead wires was not permitted. As in London, where a similar edict went forth, the undertakings were forced to adopt a different mode of current collection, and the conduit method was put in. It was not until 1942 that the last of the conduit was finally displaced.

Nowadays an extensive network is operated by two different authorities. Most urban lines are worked by the Société des Transports Intercommunaux de Bruxelles (STIB), which is also responsible for the majority of urban buses, while most of the longer lines into the outer suburbs and the surrounding districts are the province of the Société Nationale des Chemins de Fer Vicinaux (SNCV), the 'Vicinal'.

The two undertakings are of different gauges, the STIB being of standard 4 ft. 8½ in., while the Vicinal is of metre gauge. In some places in Brussels where the two services intermingle there are examples of mixed-gauge track, including complicated dual-gauge junctions which incorporate a mass of curved rails radiating in all directions so that it is a minor miracle that each car can find its right path.

For the city services the STIB employs some 600 to 800 motor trams as well as a large number of trailers.

Upper—a foretaste of things to come in Brussels; the four-track ramp leading into the subway beneath the Place de la Constitution. *(W. J. Wyse*

Lower—two types of modern tram in Brussels; left, an articulated PCC, and right a German-built articulated car. *(F. van Dam*

PLATE 11

Six-wheel trams are rare, so these modern examples in Amsterdam are particularly interesting. The small middle wheels are just visible beneath the central entrance.

(W. J. Wyse

A tramway beside a tree-lined canal could only be in Holland, and this one is in Rotterdam.

(F. van Dam

PLATE 12

One of The Hague's interurban tram routes, at its terminus in the town of Delft. The cars seen here have since been replaced by PCCs of the type shown below. *(J. Joyce)*

Representing the fine modern fleet of trams in The Hague is this PCC, seen at Scheveningen. Note the large 'picture windows'; earlier versions had small windows. *(J. Joyce)*

PLATE 13

Until recently steam trains like this were used by the Rotterdam Tramways Company. *(W. J. Wyse*

Nowadays the Rotterdam Tramways Company uses smart red-and-cream diesel trains. Here is railcar 'Swallow' with three trailers about to leave the Rotterdam terminus for Oostvoorne. *(J. Joyce*

PLATE 14

The older cars are rather box-like four-wheelers which sometimes haul a trailer of similar design. They have been considerably rebuilt since their earliest days and they are now quite fast and free-running. After about 1947 they were reconstructed with air-operated doors and without interior bulkheads, at the same time being fitted out for 'passenger flow'. The entrances were so arranged that passengers entered the motor car at the rear and the trailer at the front, so that both entrances are as close together as possible and the waiting crowds can be swallowed up quickly. An unusual feature is that there is no starting signal; the driver has tiny neon lights to indicate whether each door is open or closed, and he starts when all four lights go out.

One hundred of the more modern of these cars were rebuilt a few years ago with bodies resembling the PCC design. This was done to permit one-man operation (indicated by a '1 AGENT' board on the front) on lighter routes, and this is now being extended also to the bogie cars.

A small but interesting batch of these is the 5000 class, of which there are only 25. These are of the more classical type, but are noted for their smooth running and high speed. They have been the subject of a good deal of modification, including new bodies of PCC style.

In contrast to these older members of the fleet are the true PCC's. The first of these were introduced in 1951 and they now number some 150 in all. The trucks and equipment are of American design, but were made in Belgium under licence, the bogies being of typical PCC type with inside frames and with rubber inserts in the wheels. The electrical equipment is planned to give smooth and rapid acceleration; four motors of 55 horse power each enable speeds of over 40 miles an hour to be attained.

Electric power is also used for the braking. Rheostatic braking (in which the motors act as generators to dissipate current in heating the resistances) is employed for normal service stops. Magnetic track brakes (which appear as great blocks hanging down between the wheels of each truck, each block forming part of an electro-magnet which can be energised to cling to the steel rails) can bring the car to a dead stand in dramatic fashion in an emergency, so drastic in fact that passengers can almost be thrown through the front window in a sudden halt.

Another safety measure is the graphically named 'dead man's pedal'. This has to be held down by the motorman with his left foot all the time the car is running, for if he releases it the car will automatically come to a stop. Such a device (although generally hand operated) has long been common on electric trains, but its employment on tramcars is a comparatively recent development and is a reflection of the high speed of the modern vehicle.

If the 'works' of the PCC are American, the body itself – although using American constructional principles – is of Belgian design to meet local needs. In appearance it is of pleasing streamlined shape, with tapering ends and a sloping windscreen. It is over 46 feet long, and like all Brussels trams it is single-ended with a driving position at one end only and doors on one side.

There are three doorways, each with power-operated folding doors. The rear doorway is used as the entrance, while the other two – at centre and front respectively – are the exits. The conductor has a seat and a cash desk just inside the entrance. The boarding and fare-paying process is speeded up by the fact that (with minor exceptions) the 'flat' fare is the same for any distance, while there are also multi-ride and season tickets to make the job of the conductor easier and quicker.

Further, as again is normal practice on the Continent but not in Britain, there is plenty of standing room. Although there are only about 30 seats in the PCC, there is space for about another 70 standing, with the result that the total load of some 100 compares favourably with a typical British double-deck bus with its 70 or so, and of course it can be loaded and unloaded more quickly through the three doors.

Now the STIB has gone a stage further by constructing a small group of articulated cars from older four-wheelers. These are of the 'two rooms and a bath' type (that is, with two long end sections joined by a short centre section) and are considered a stop-gap until new vehicles are ordered under the modernisation plan. An experimental articulated PCC has also been introduced.

While new rolling stock has been coming on the scene, developments have been taking place in the routes on which it runs. Half a dozen extensions were made in the years between 1947 and 1951, including new sections to Drogenbos in 1947 and to Neerpede and Grand-Bigard in 1948. One of the most striking transformations of recent years has been the transfer of whole sections of line from the streets to their own reserved tracks, notably in the wide boulevards that encircle the city.

Much of this work occurred in preparation for the great exhibition of 1958, which was held in the northern suburb of Heysel. The object was not only to provide for the large amount of additional traffic expected in the streets, but also to cater for the enormous number of visitors who would need public transport to the exhibition.

At the same time the opportunity was taken to carry out plans which would have a long-term effect in improving traffic conditions in the capital. The work included motorways in the heart of the city as well as such spectacular structures as viaducts, and improvements to private and public transport went hand-in-hand.

Instead of making these developments a reason for getting rid of the trams, the new layouts were in fact designed for them. One example of this is along the Boulevard d'Anvers; here there is a long viaduct for road traffic, while beneath there are four tramway tracks, two for local services and two for interurbans.

By such means, public transport has been to a large extent segregated from the flow of lorries and cars along the streets, to the benefit of all. This not only enables traffic to flow free from such vehicles as buses, but also gives the trams an unobstructed course without being impeded by other traffic;

if buses were used for public transport they could not be separated in this way, but would have to mingle with the mass of other vehicles. By segregating public transport, services can be maintained with a speed and regularity that would otherwise be impossible in the crowded streets.

The latest development will be even more drastic – putting the trams underground. Here they are removed from the streets altogether and located in tunnels underneath, so that they become in effect underground railways. The idea is not new – London and Boston had such tunnels 50 years ago – but it has come to the fore again in recent years and more will be heard of it in the future.

Have a look at the main subway in Brussels. Opened in 1957, it is quite short but is a sample of what is to come; it is situated near the Midi station and runs beneath the wide Place de la Constitution. The principal part carries four tracks and there is a station with four platforms. There are four entrances to the subway by means of ramps, the most impressive of which also has four tracks as well as the platforms of a station. The subway is brightly lit throughout, while the underground station is reached from the street by five entrances, two of them with escalators. There are two underground junctions.

The total length of the subway, including its approach ramps, is over half a mile. It is used by more than 3,500 trams a day, carrying some 200,000 passengers in speed and safety away from the congestion of the streets.

But this is only the beginning of the future plan. It is intended that further subways should be constructed to take trams underground in other busy central districts. Nearly 12 miles of tunnels would allow trams to be removed from the surface altogether in the centre, while in the suburbs they would as far as possible operate on reserved tracks. Routes which did not fit into this scheme would be replaced by buses, and the layout of the tunnels would be such that they could be adapted to accommodate full-size underground trains at some future time if necessary.

X

Dutch Trilogy
(Amsterdam, The Hague, Rotterdam)

HOLLAND is a small country and you might expect its three tramway systems to be much alike. But in fact they are quite different – in character, in routes and rolling stock, and even in livery.

Amsterdam is known in the guide books as the 'Venice of the north'. It is a city of canals, bridges and narrow streets, while it also has all the bustle of commerce. The Hague by contrast is the dignified royal city, with its palace and its Government offices, wide avenues and more leisurely atmosphere. Rotterdam is one of the busiest ports of Europe, with a character reflected in the fine modern buildings and the reconstructed central area where tramways run on reservations in the middle of wide streets.

The liveries of the three undertakings are also distinctive. There is the sober grey of Amsterdam, the dignified cream of The Hague, and the business-like yellow of Rotterdam.

However, one thing they have in common is modernity, and many interesting features show the integration of the tramway into present-day conditions. But even here there are differences, for the modern cars chosen by the three are again quite distinctive, as though each had decided that it would go as far as it could to assert its individuality and to show that it had no connection with the town next door.

Look at examples from the three undertakings, each put into service at about the same time during the later 1950s.

Amsterdam's choice is an articulated car running on three bogies and nearly 60 feet long. It is in two sections, pivoted in the middle but with a clear passage throughout its entire length. There are large doors at the rear for the entrance, while there are three exits, two near the middle and one at the front. There are seats for 40 passengers and room for over a hundred standing. Externally the outline is smooth and the ends rounded, while the fairing is brought down low so that it almost hides the wheels.

Not content with this design they have now gone one better and introduced a three-section version running on four bogies. This giant and its later fellows can carry over 200 passengers.

The Hague seems to have been inspired by American influence in its modern trams, for they are of the PCC type that was familiar in the United States. This is a bogie vehicle with a curved swept-down front, the first of the class being extremely American in appearance, even to the multitude of small windows which were by no means popular with Dutch passengers. Later vehicles were modified with large 'picture windows' and this version has been adopted as standard.

Most of these PCC's have the entrance at the front, while the exits are at the centre and rear. Seats are provided for 36 passengers, although the total load is as much as 100. The later cars are arranged so that they can be coupled together for multiple-unit operation in pairs at busy times, thus giving a high-capacity unit that makes the most economical use of road space.

Unusually, they are equipped for one-man operation, passengers paying the driver as they enter, a method making for further economy. The success of this with the first experiments led to its wide-scale adoption, and there are now over 150 of this type altogether.

Like Amsterdam, Rotterdam favours the articulated car, but its design is different in appearance. It has a more angular outline and although the entrance is again at the rear, there are two exits near the front part. The whole vehicle is over 60 feet long and has a capacity of nearly 200.

Although so dissimilar, all three types have certain features in common. They all use the pantograph for current collection, they all have power-operated folding doors to give maximum safety for passengers boarding and alighting, and they are all single-ended.

These modern streamliners make an interesting contrast with older fleets of the same undertakings. They indicate how far design has progressed in recent years.

Earlier rolling stock in The Hague and Amsterdam consisted of four-wheelers hauling trailers, the typical Continental unit of the past. In Rotterdam the older vehicles had central entrances, but they were found to be too slow in loading and unloading.

A contrast can also be made with an earlier design in Amsterdam, in this case one introduced in the post-war years from 1948 to 1950. These cars are remarkable in that they are six-wheelers, with a smaller pair of wheels beneath the centre of the body between the main wheels. There are similar trailers to match the motors, and each can carry about 80 passengers. Again the 'pay as you enter' method of fare collection is employed, coming into general use for the first time with this new design after having previously been confined to a few one-man-worked trams.

Now look at the routes on which these streamliners operate. In Amsterdam the focal point of the system is the Central Station, where there are loops around the station forecourt. There are several tracks here with appropriate loading points for the various routes.

From this centre the lines radiate out to east, south and west, after traversing some of the main streets. The network is completed by two heavily-loaded circumferential routes which form two 'middle circles' quite close to each other. Double track predominates, in some cases making use of one-way streets with 'up' and 'down' tracks in adjacent thoroughfares. Islands are provided at stops to protect passengers getting on and off.

Two smaller features may appear unusual to the visitor. First, you can see the odd sight of someone posting a letter on a tram. A post-box is hung at the back of the car, and at the Central Station you can see these being emptied by the postman with his sack. Second is the use of colour codes on the destination indicators to show the routes, and these give a pleasant dash of colour to the front of the car.

There have been apparent contradictions in the story of recent developments in Amsterdam. In 1954 a new tramway was opened to serve the growing suburb of Slotermeer to the west of the city. But then in the following year certain other routes were closed; these ran through some of the narrower streets, however, so their closure was not unexpected.

More recently though has come the real surprise. In 1962 a brand-new line was opened to the new suburb of Osdorp, a high-speed route entirely on its own right-of-way and with stops about half a mile apart. Speeds are high, as the newest cars are employed for the service.

Strangely enough the opening of this three-mile extension also involved the reinstatement of a tram route that had been replaced by buses. This was to allow the new line to be connected to the rest of the system. Truly trams have made a comeback in Amsterdam!

This is hardly less true of The Hague, where the modern system is operated by the Hague Tramways Company (HTM). The layout is fairly compact, with bus routes supplementing rather than paralleling. The spacious thoroughfares make it possible to have loading islands and reservations in many places and good use is made of squares and odd pieces of land in order to provide a right of way, while in the suburbs this form of layout is generously installed wherever possible.

A tour of the system also shows another feature that assists in the retention of the tramways. There are tall blocks of flats that are typical of modern Dutch urban architecture. From the transport point of view these have the advantage of maintaining a high density of population in a limited area; this provides good patronage along a short route, making conditions favourable to the continuance of tramways which require a heavy traffic to justify the cost of their fixed equipment.

This contrasts with the situation in Britain, where the common succession of semi-detached houses with gardens means that towns sprawl into extensive suburbs with a comparatively low density of population; transport routes therefore have to be long and often lightly loaded, at least at the outer ends.

An out-of-the-ordinary route in The Hague is the No. 11. Indeed if you travel on it you would not be far wrong in thinking it a railway rather than a tramway, for it was a steam branch line until it was taken over and electrified in 1927.

Its city terminus is almost within the Hollandse Spoor main-line station, and from there it is entirely on its own right of way, often apart from the streets altogether as it passes power stations, gas works and backyards. All the way it appears so inextricably mixed up with real railway lines that it comes as no surprise to see cream-coloured steeple-cab electric locomotives hauling Netherlands Railways wagons along the same tracks as the trams.

This former branch line now carries a heavy traffic and a frequent service. One reason is that it traverses a densely populated district. Another reason is that its out-of-town end reaches an area of quite a different sort, for it suddenly emerges on to the seafront at the popular resort of Scheveningen. Here there is a turning circle adjoining the promenade.

Scheveningen can also be reached from The Hague by two other routes of more conventional style, and these also are well patronised, particularly at holiday times. A favourite spot is the famous Kuurhaus, in front of which the trams are to be seen constantly gliding around the terminal loops.

Until a few years ago there were also several interurban routes around The Hague. Two of these went by different ways to the town of Leiden; one was worked by the HTM, the other by the NZH (the North South Holland Transport Company). The HTM used heavy centre-entrance vehicles, while the NZH blue trams included articulated examples which were virtually the prototypes for present-day European practice.

Both these lines have been replaced by buses, but two other interurbans have been given a new lease of life. These are the routes to Voorburg and Delft, which used to be worked by the HTM with its centre-entrance cars; now with the introduction of the fleet of PCC's these have taken over to provide fast service to these outlying districts. Delft of course is famous for its china, and the swift glide on the PCC across the fields from The Hague is a pleasant way for the visitor to reach this picturesque old town.

If Delft is old-world in atmosphere, Rotterdam is noted for its modern architecture. Much of the central area destroyed during the war has since been rebuilt in the most up-to-date manner.

Not only are there modern trams to blend with these surroundings, but the tracks have been incorporated into the street layout as it has been rebuilt. In the important thoroughfare of the Coolsingel, for example, they are laid on a reservation in the centre of a dual carriageway, while at the busy junction of the Hoffplein there is a vast roundabout. Many suburban routes, too, incorporate lengths of reserved tracks.

Rotterdam is a port and the trams serve the dock areas on such routes as those to Delfshaven and Schiedam. Docks and shipyards line the River Maas along which the city is built, and while the major part is on the north side, several routes cross the river to serve the districts to the south.

This is where one of the physical difficulties of the layout can be observed, for all these routes have to cross one bridge, the Willemsbrug, which also has to carry a great amount of road traffic in spite of the nearby tunnel under the river. Moreover, the Willemsbrug is an opening bridge that has to be raised to allow shipping through.

This bottleneck can play havoc with the services, as well as with other traffic. Hence plans have been drawn up to improve the position, and with the anticipated growth in the city and its traffic in coming years, an underground railway is envisaged. This will go under the river to serve the southern districts, and its coming will cause reconstruction of the tramways in this part of the system.

An unusual sight south of the river is the diesel tramway of the Rotterdam Tramway Company (RTM), a completely different organisation from the city undertaking. The RTM operates lines which are really narrow gauge light railways, rather than street tramways, extending from Rotterdam to the villages of Hellevoetsluis and Oostvoorne. The 'trams' consist of diesel railcars hauling trailers as necessary. On leaving the city terminus at Rosestraat they run adjacent to the streets, and even mingle with the electric cars in places, although they cannot use the same tracks for they are of 3 ft. 6 in. gauge instead of the urban lines' standard gauge.

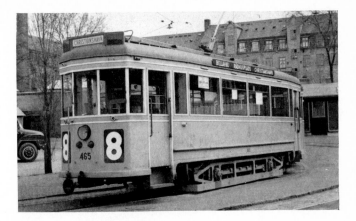

Three generations of Copenhagen tramcar illustrate the development from traditional four-wheeler to the bogie car and the articulated car.

(Jan Walter

PLATE 15

A contrast in Copenhagen: upper, an early double-decker with its unusual half-enclosed top deck, and, lower, a modern German-design articulated car on the sightseeing service.

(Jan Walter

PLATE 16

Wuppertal's 'trams in the sky'. Trains on the famous monorail or 'Schwebebahn' speed above the streets of Vohwinkel. *(J. Bazin*

In earlier days four-wheelers like these were typical of German tramways. These two are seen at Iserlohn on the extensive Rhine-Ruhr network. *(W. J. Wyse*

PLATE 17

The modern German tramway: upper, a tramway station in Essen, complete with shelters and escalators. Centre, a glimpse of the Essen–Mülheim rapid-transit tramway. Note the subway. Lower, is this the longest tram? A three-section articulated car in Düsseldorf.

(W. J. Wyse

PLATE 18

XI

Wonderful Copenhagen

ONE particularly treasured museum piece in Copenhagen vividly recalls the origins of public transport in the Danish capital. This is tram No. 419, which not only towers high above all the others but is of a shape that looks somehow familiar to British eyes. No. 419 dates from the turn of the century, and like so many typically British trams it is a double-decker, a fact so uncommon on the Continent as to cause immediate comment.

But the outline of this double-decker is not exactly like that of its British contemporaries. To begin with, the top deck is half enclosed and half open, as though the builders had run out of materials before they had completed their job. The front half of the top has sides with windows and roof, but the rear half is open from the waistline up. British trams were often completely open on top or else entirely enclosed, while some even had the middle enclosed and both ends open, but none had quite this arrangement.

However, this exhibit is a link with the earliest days of the system, for it was a British company that first introduced trams to the Copenhagen area. And so it was not surprising that they brought with them something of their native land and that for many years thereafter the Danes had the pleasure of travelling along the streets on such an elevated perch.

The first line was opened as long ago as 1863. Extensions were soon made, and other companies came on the scene, until by the 1890s there were half a dozen different companies employing more than 200 horse cars. Both steam and battery electric traction were also tried, but neither proved to be successful, and in 1899 electric operation using overhead wires began.

It was at this time that the family of which surviving 419 is a member was introduced. At first these double-deckers had their upper decks entirely open, but apparently the breeze generated by the high speed of these fast mechanical monsters was too much for the Copenhagers, so the front half of the top was given a roof in order that at least the first-comers could have some protection even if the others still had to endure the elements. The cars were single-ended, so there was a stairway at one end only.

These unsymmetrical vehicles belonged to the Frederiksberg Tramways Company, which operated its lines in the area of that town lying to the west of Copenhagen. Another company, the Copenhagen Tramways, this time within the capital itself, was also a supporter of the double-decker, but it favoured more conventional vehicles with two staircases and completely enclosed top deck. These, however, were later converted to single-deckers, whereas half-and-half No. 419 remained in service until 1935.

Both undertakings were later acquired by the municipality, the Copenhagen company in 1911 and the Frederiksberg company in 1919. By the start of the 1920s there were some 900 trams, in about equal numbers of motors and trailers. Then came a decade of expansion, as new lines were built to serve the growing suburbs of the city. Extension was made to Vanlose in 1922, and lengthy routes were laid to Husum and to Soborg in 1924.

The 1930s saw the introduction of a large batch of new cars to meet the need for more up-to-date rolling stock on the expanding network. Some 190 bogie single-deckers took the road to bring a marked improvement on the early four-wheelers. Externally the most striking feature of these newcomers was the layout of the large windows, which were in three 'bays' each with one wide and two narrow panes. At the same time, many of the older units were rejuvenated, while during the war years 'austerity' cars were constructed utilising parts from old vehicles.

Something completely new appeared in 1949, when the first of the post-war tramcars was put into service. Like its predecessors this was mounted on bogies, but it was graced with more modern lines and a somewhat angular streamlined end design. Numbered 701, it was the prototype of a batch of eight in the years to 1952. Each was 46 feet long and carried 90 passengers.

The important departure from previous practice in this new class was the use of passenger flow. It was soon found that this reduced the total number of uncollected fares and so resulted in an increase in revenue. Accordingly, its use was later extended to many of the older bogie cars.

Even more dramatic has been the latest development in rolling stock. In 1957–58 experiments were made with an articulated car on loan from Düsseldorf in Germany. This had a capacity of 150 passengers, so that it was comparable with an ordinary unit of motor plus trailer, yet required a crew of only two insead of three. With rising wage costs this was a significant factor in the economics of operation.

Moreover, the articulated vehicle, although 63 feet long, is some 20 feet shorter than an equivalent bogie motor and trailer. It is therefore able to make more economical use of the road space, a major point in the narrow streets that are becoming increasingly congested.

The result of the experiment with the German 'artic' was so successful that a fleet of 100 was put on order.

Copenhagen today has a population approaching 1½ million, having spread into numerous suburbs in the surrounding area. The trams serve most of the heavily built-up districts, but since no new routes have been constructed since the war, all new development is served by buses. The bus fleet has thus grown considerably; its increasing importance is seen by the fact that it carried as many as 13 per cent of the undertaking's total number of passengers in 1953–54 compared with only 7 per cent in 1938–39.

In some cases the buses act as feeders to the trams, but in others they have replaced some of the lightly loaded routes.

An indication of the changing pattern of services, both in total demand and in the different forms of transport, can be observed in these figures which show the number of passengers carried:

Year	Tram	Bus	Trolleybus	Total
1938–39	142 million	10 million	2 million	154 million
1953–54	177 million	26 million	3 million	206 million
1958–59	134 million	37 million	3 million	174 million

The fleet in 1959 consisted of 840 trams (including 375 trailers), 213 buses and 13 trolleybuses. Of the tram fleet, some two-thirds was over 40 years old, so it was obvious that the question of replacement was one of some urgency; since then buses have taken over certain routes while new trams have also been introduced.

For the immediate future the trams are likely to remain as the principal form of transport on the main radial routes of the city, where a frequent service of high-capacity vehicles is required. It looks as though half a dozen cross-town routes may continue for perhaps 20 years until the coming of a proposed underground railway which will again bring substantial alteration to the pattern.

Like so many other cities nowadays, Copenhagen is plagued with traffic congestion, which has the effect of slowing public transport, while at the same time it suffers from the increasing use of private cars as a competitor. There are many narrow streets, while the number of bridges creates further bottlenecks.

One local factor is the great use of bicycles. This not only affects the traffic carried on public transport – more people cycle in good weather than in bad – but it also affects the efficiency of the different types of transport.

With almost continuous flows of bicycles along the streets, there is much to be said for the tram running on its fixed tracks in the middle of the thoroughfare rather than the bus which has to pull into the kerb at stops. Not only is the weaving action of the bus dangerous to cyclists, but it even has difficulty in getting into the kerb through the stream of cyclists, so that its overall speed may be lower than that of the tram.

To many, Copenhagen means the Little Mermaid and the Tivoli, for the city is well known on the tourist's itinerary. To cater for this the transport authority operates special sightseeing trams which make a circular tour of the city. The cars used on this service are prominently labelled for the benefit of the traveller; to local folk they are 'Turistsporvogn', while the English visitor can equally understand when he sees the word 'Sightseeing' emblazoned on the side in large letters.

XII

The World's Greatest Network
(The Ruhr)

THROUGH the towns of the Ruhr – the heart of industrial Germany – stretches the world's greatest tramway network. Linking such busy centres as Düsseldorf, Essen, Mülheim and Duisburg, the tracks extend for mile after mile across this vast conurbation. Once, Britain had networks of comparable extent, but they were nothing like this, and if you go there you are likely to be in for some surprises.

Formerly the network was held together with long rural lines that did not have sufficient traffic to ensure their survival to the present day. But there is still a close mesh of routes comprising the systems of Bochum-Gelsenkirchen, Essen, Mülheim, Oberhausen, Duisburg, Düsseldorf and Krefeld, while to the north is the sprawling Vestische system.

You can go by tram (if you have enough time and patience) from any one to any other, and services are often provided jointly by several operators. In Essen, for example, you can see trams from Oberhausen, Mülheim and Bochum, as well as those of the home town. In Mülheim you can see 'foreigners' from Duisburg, Oberhausen and Essen.

Many of them look much the same, for the popular livery is cream with a coloured band. In Essen, Bochum and Duisburg this coloured band is green, while Mülheim favours blue-green and Oberhausen light blue. By contrast, the Vestische has adopted an all-over green. But apart from the colour, you can identify a car by other characteristics; Mülheim cars are immaculate, without advertisements, and silent, Oberhausen is fond of three-axle cars, while Essen drivers use their warning bells as though they were driving fire engines.

There are other tramways a short distance away from the main group. Hagen and Wuppertal are to the south, and Wuppertal is joined to Remscheid. To the north east, Dortmund operates cars in different shades of chocolate on fast suburban routes.

Two gauges are to be found in this extensive network. Most of the towns favoured the metre gauge, but standard was adopted in Düsseldorf and Duisburg and in places the metre gauge has been converted to standard. In some towns – including Duisburg, Düsseldorf and Wuppertal – the two gauges could be seen together.

A little further away up the River Rhine is Cologne, which has a tramway par excellence. Here are four-car 'trains' running into the country on magnificent railway-like tracks complete with such embellishments as level crossing gates. There are also heavy interurbans on two routes to the Federal capital of Bonn, 17 miles south of Cologne.

If you expect to find the Ruhr a region of unmitigated gloom or one unrelieved 'Black Country' you will be pleasantly surprised. Certainly there are factories and steelworks, but equally there are expanses of countryside that would not look out of place in Surrey. And the towns and cities themselves have largely been rebuilt since the war, with well-laid-out centres and modern buildings.

The trams are in keeping with the modernity of their surroundings. All over the area you will find big spacious articulated cars which glide smoothly and swiftly through the street and along the suburban reservations.

Such is the case in Düsseldorf, a city of some 600,000 inhabitants. In its centre there is a modern tram station at the Jan Willem Platz and another with four tracks in front of the main railway station. In the suburbs there are miles of reserved tracks, a species of layout that has been widely adopted in recent years where development and reconstruction have taken place. The system is operated by the Rheinische Bahngesellschaft, or 'Rheinbahn', which works a total length of routes amounting to around 130 miles.

Düsseldorf is the home of the German articulated tram, and this type comprised more than one-third of the total fleet of about 300 motors in mid-1964. Düsseldorf is the location of the 'Waggonfabrik Uerdingen, Werk Düsseldorf' where the famous Düwag trams are built. The name Düwag is synonymous with the modern German bogie and articulated cars, though this concern is not the only builder of them.

They symbolise the transformation that has taken place since pre-war days when the four-wheeler hauling one or more similar trailers was the typical rolling stock of German tramways. During the war the 'Kriegs Strassenbahnwagen' (KSW), or wartime 'austerity' tram, was introduced as a replacement when needed; this was again a four-wheeler, although of more refined appearance. The KSW was designed in 1942–43 and over 650 of the same basic pattern were constructed until 1951, destined for several different towns.

Satisfactory though it was as a makeshift, the KSW could hardly be regarded as the ultimate, and in the post-war period more up-to-date equipment was called for. Hence in 1950 a committee was set up to formulate plans for a vehicle of more advanced design but of a standardised type that could be produced in quantity at a reasonable price. This committee included representatives of the country's tramcar builders as well as the several undertakings who were interested in acquiring new stock; these included Cologne, Dortmund, Duisburg, Düsseldorf, Hanover and Wuppertal.

As a result of these deliberations the first of the now famous Düwag cars was delivered in 1951. Built in Düsseldorf to the order of Hanover, it was a bogie streamliner capable of carrying 100 passengers and hauling a matching trailer. A second set, differing only in detail, was delivered soon afterwards to the Düsseldorf lines.

In appearance the newcomer was of pleasing shape, with rounded ends and a sloping windscreen. It was 46 feet long and had a rear entrance with front and middle exits fitted with electrically-operated doors. It was single-ended and was provided with a conductor's desk at the entrance for 'pay as you enter' fare collection. The car was capable of a speed of 37 miles an hour, and had electric braking and resilient wheels.

There could be little doubt of the success of a venture marking such an advance on tradition. In the next few years cars of this general design were to be seen on most of the German systems that were intent on modernising, helping in many places to swing the balance in favour of retaining the tramways. Now even more modern articulated cars have been developed and these are already to be seen in large numbers.

Among all these, you will find in Düsseldorf the most unlikely item of tramway rolling stock – a restaurant car. The idea of being able to sit at a table and take soup, sausage or coffee while travelling along the street in a tram seems the height of incongruity. Yet you can do just that if you ride the interurban route from Düsseldorf to Duisburg.

Known as the 'D-Bahn', this interurban uses cars owned by the under-takings of the two towns it serves, but they are distinguished from the more mundane vehicles by having red bands instead of the usual colour. These great three-section 'artics' have a small kitchen and refreshment section in their middle part, and here the hungry traveller can eat *en route*.

The Düsseldorf terminus of this 16-mile-long 'D-Bahn' is in Jan Willem Platz. From here it traverses the streets for a short distance before entering first a four-track reservation and then private right of way on which it continues nearly all the way to Duisburg, where it terminates at Saarstrasse.

Although so impressive now, it did not start life in such a grandiose fashion. It originated in 1900 when little four-wheelers began a leisurely journey on single track laid at the side of the narrow roads between the two towns.

Transformation came about when this 'Kleinbahn' was acquired by the undertakings of Düsseldorf and Duisburg in 1926. They quickly set about the task of making it into something much more imposing. They cut a new right of way across country to by-pass the roads, laid two tracks throughout, and introduced more modern bogie rolling stock.

There is also another interurban out of Düsseldorf, the 'K-Bahn', this time running on the west bank of the Rhine a distance of about 13 miles to the town of Krefeld. Nowadays it is worked by heavy three-section 250-passenger 'artics'; these were rebuilt from more conventional stock which formed sets of three, one of which was a restaurant car on certain trains. The first 'diner' was introduced as long ago as 1926, but since the present vehicles have to 'double' on short-workings intermingled with their longer runs, this facility has now disappeared, leaving the 'D-Bahn' unique in

Germany in this respect. However, even if you cannot eat on them, you will find that the Krefeld cars have a remarkable turn of speed when necessary, especially on the long rural section.

While you are in the Ruhr area, you should certainly not miss seeing the famous 'upside down railway' of Wuppertal – or the 'Schwebebahn' to give it its proper title. For more than sixty years this monorail has been speeding its passengers through the air from Oberbarmen to Barmen, Elberfeld and Vohwinkel along the valley of the River Wupper.

Imagine a pair of coupled single-deck trams with their trucks above the roof, but with one wheel per axle instead of two, and you have some idea of what a Schwebebahn train looks like. There is plenty of variety, with the original cars of 1901 still running, smart streamliners of 1950, and a blue and silver articulated set which follows the trend of the modern tram.

The trains hang from rails on the edge of an elevated platform slung from A-section supports every 100 feet or so. The stations are also carried by these supports, with platforms up in the air. There is no notice to tell you not to cross the line from one platform to the other, but there is a sheet of wire netting between them to remind you not to try it. And to stop you falling out into the river, the trains have air-operated doors that have to be locked by the driver before he can start.

For most of its way the line follows the course of the river, which is anything but straight. There are severe speed restrictions on the many curves, and if these are not carefully observed, centrifugal force makes itself felt and the cars swing outward and sway alarmingly.

At the Vohwinkel end, the line forsakes the river and follows the main street, where it is carried from huge inverted U supports. What the people who live on the first and second floors have to say about the trains that roar past their bedroom windows is not recorded, but at least these trams in the sky are never delayed by traffic jams.

XIII

By The Blue Danube
(Vienna)

WHO could have resisted a ride on the 'Emperor Franz Joseph I Horse Tram'? That was the splendidly regal title of the first line in the Austrian capital. It started just one hundred years ago, in 1865, and even if there is nothing at present so majestically named, Vienna can now boast the largest tram fleet in the world, with a total of about 2,300 to rival the 2,600 of London in its heyday.

Look at some of the impressive figures. As far back as 1903 there were over 100 miles of route and 158 million passengers were carried in the year. In 1913 the route mileage had shot up to 150, while the number of passengers had soared to 325 million. In the years from 1907 to 1914 forty-five miles of new routes were added to the network.

In 1936 there were 68 different services operating on 178 miles of lines. The total stock available was no fewer than 3,300 and in the course of that year 409 million passengers were carried. In some of the main streets as many as 100 trams an hour passed by in the morning peak.

The fleet in 1955 included over 1,300 motors and about the same number of trailers. To these figures had to be added another 150 motors and 220 trailers of the underground railway, or Stadtbahn, for these vehicles are almost identical with the street tramcars. Over 500 million passengers were carried in a year on 63 services covering a route length of 165 miles.

The first trams were hauled by horses, but in 1883 mechanical traction was inaugurated when a steam-worked line was brought into use. An experimental electric section was opened in 1897, by which time there were no fewer than 980 trams in the city, and in the following year two further routes were electrified. Such was the success of the new method of traction that electrification went ahead by leaps and bounds, with the inevitable outcome that by 1903 Vienna was saying goodbye to the last of the horses, in the same year that the network was taken over by the municipal authorities.

No trams have penetrated the narrow streets of the old parts of the inner areas of Vienna. But outside this the tramways follow the famous thoroughfare of the Ring, which is a wide boulevard surrounding the centre of the city and laid on the site of the old fortifications.

The general pattern of the system is that outside this hole in the middle the routes radiate outward from the Ring in nearly all directions, while

At the interurban terminus at Jan Willem Platz in Düsseldorf. An older train on the service to Krefeld on the left stands side by side with a new articulated car on the Duisburg service. *(P. Malterre*

'Speisewagen' is a rare legend to find on a tram. This is a tramway restaurant car on the interurban route between Düsseldorf and Krefeld. *(W. J. Wyse*

PLATE 19

Representative of modern rolling stock on the Vienna tramways is this three-section articulated car.

(R. James

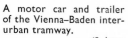

A motor car and trailer of the Vienna–Baden interurban tramway.

(R. James

A train on the Vienna 'Stadtbahn' looks just like a string of tramcars coupled together.

(R. James

PLATE 20

Above – an ex-New York tram in service in Vienna.
(*R. James*

Right – a bird's-eye view of an older type of Moscow tram and trailer.
(*Hugh Ballment*

PLATE 21

A contrast in Alexandria; a modern motor car mounted on ex-London trucks passes an old-type motor car and trailer.

(N. N. Forbes

A line-up of stock on the Alexandria and Ramleh tramway at the Ramleh terminus, including a double-decker.

(Hugh Ballment

PLATE 22

others connect the radial ones. Vienna is a hilly city and many gradients have to be negotiated.

Rolling stock was anything but standard, but generally it comprised typical Continental four-wheelers hauling trailers. One of the features of this vast fleet has been the fact that many of the old cars have had an extremely long life, so that it has been possible to see 80-year-old former steam trailers still in service side by side with the modern streamliners.

Partly this longevity was necessitated by wartime conditions, when the acquisition of new rolling stock had to be deferred while at the same time serious damage was suffered. During the Second World War over 580 trams were totally destroyed. In this period, as well as during the First World War, freight services were operated over the tramways. When hostilities ceased, recovery went ahead as speedily as possible, and already by the end of 1945 now fewer than 35 of the routes were again in commission.

The need for additional rolling stock at this hectic time led to some American visitors coming to help out; these took the shape of 45 cars of the Third Avenue Transit Company of New York. With their characteristic American 'streetcar' look they brought a touch of the new world to central Europe, but their extreme width limited them to only a few routes.

In the post-war years an enormous number of new or modernised cars have been introduced, and the latest types bear comparison with any to be found elsewhere.

The new designs have included the type B introduced in 1950 and amounting to fifty in all. These are smart vehicles with seats for 20 passengers and room for some 50 standing, and they haul trailers of a similar pattern. Another batch, built under German licence, consists of a number of 'Grossraumwagen', which are typical of modern German practice with three sets of doors and pay-as-you-enter fare collection. These vehicles also carry about 70 passengers and run with similar trailers.

The latest pattern is a two-section articulated type, capable of carrying more than 150 passengers. Like so many contemporary trams, it is arranged for pay-as-you-enter operation, with separate entrances and exits fitted with power-operated doors.

The prototype of one articulated design, No. 4301, was cunningly created from two of the old Stadtbahn trailers. But, like so many post-war rebuilds, so well was the job done that no one would know from its appearance that the result was not an entirely new construction. It consists in effect of two four-wheelers linked together by a short centre section, and it has pleasantly smooth contours with rounded ends and curved windscreens. The complete vehicle has a length of almost 70 feet and a weight of about 25 tons. Although there are seats for only 30, there is ample room for 90 standing, making the total capacity as high as 120.

Since the war a total of more than 400 motors and 600 trailers has been put into service, replacing much of the antiquated rolling stock. The total fleet now numbers some 1,100 motors and over 1,200 trailers.

Indicative of present-day developments is a new layout that was opened at the busy terminus at the Schottentor in 1961. This is on two levels. A ramp from the street leads down into a subway where there is a sub-surface turning loop used by four routes, while on the surface another loop is used by two other routes.

Further subways are planned in the central areas to ease the flow of traffic at the most congested points. One subway will break new ground by crossing the hitherto tram-free centre. A good deal of re-alignment of tracks has also been undertaken, while in the suburbs some of the routes have been extended to serve new residential districts.

An odd part of the undertaking is the Stadtbahn, or underground railway. Once a steam-worked railway, it is strange in that it is operated by tramcars coupled into trains; to make confusion worse confounded these 'trains' used to leave their railway and wander off through the streets as trams.

This strange state of affairs occurred in pre-war years, when the underground train behaved as a normal train for its journey from Heiligenstadt to Gumpendorfer Strasse, but here it entered the streets and ran as a tram to the south station. This versatile service was not resumed after the war as, not surprisingly, it was found that a train that might be delayed by traffic when parading along the street was likely to cause chaos to the working of the real railway. However, even today you can sometimes see the all-red Stadtbahn cars working as trams, although not in eight-car trains!

Also worth looking out for is the interurban tramway which runs south from Vienna to the town of Baden. This had its origins in steam days, but through electric working began in 1907 and now substantial bogie cars are employed on this 'Lokalbahn'.

XIV

No Tram to Red Square
(Moscow)

YOU might visit Moscow without even seeing any trams, for they have
been banished from the centre of the city. Narrow streets in the old
areas were considered unsuitable for the continuance of tramway operation,
while many wide thoroughfares have been provided with trolleybuses. This
form of transport has been given special emphasis in these districts, where
the fumes and noise of the motor bus were undesirable, and the trolleybus
fleet now numbers more than 1,000 and is the largest in the world.

At the same time the underground railways have been extended to cope
with the most intensive traffic, in many cases resulting in the abandonment
of the tramways that followed paralleling routes. The first line of the underground or Metro was opened in 1935, and the system now amounts to over
60 miles with more extensions planned or under construction.

What, then, is left for the trams to do? Quite a lot; so much, indeed, that
a fleet of about 1,800 is needed. Although they have been removed from the
centre, they still operate long lines into the suburbs, and in some cases they
have been extended in recent years to meet new housing development.

The network today has an unusual shape. The most obvious feature is a
large gap in the middle, making it rather reminiscent of the situation in
London. The heart of the city is Red Square, and from this nucleus roads
radiate outward in all directions, with such thoroughfares as the fabulously
wide Gorki Street carrying swiftly gliding trolleybuses.

About a mile out from the centre is the inner circular road, and this
is the nearest that the trams now penetrate to the heart. Other termini
are even farther out, while there are also circumferential routes that encircle
the centre at a considerable distance.

Once they get started the trams run for several miles into the vast suburbs
of Moscow, in certain cases being laid on reserved tracks. Although they
are often paralleled by bus or trolleybus services, they primarily act as
feeders to the underground railways and provide high-capacity transport
to those districts which the underground has not yet reached.

If the tramways thus have something of the function of suburban railways,
this impression may be heightened by the appearance of some of the older
rolling stock. This includes large and heavy bogie vehicles, tall and rather
angular and hauling trailers. Like the rest of the fleet they are arranged

for single-ended operation, as each terminus has a turning loop. The bogie cars number some 250, while in addition there are many four-wheelers which again have been rebuilt as single-enders.

In contrast to these are the more modern cars. The first of a new type which appeared in 1937 was a streamliner with a vague affinity to the American PCC. Its body styling incorporated a centre entrance and front exit, while other refinements included electric heating and the use of rubber in the springing to give smoother riding. This vehicle had seats for 54 passengers and could reach a speed of over 35 miles an hour.

Other streamliners appeared before the war, while after the war a modernised version was brought out. Over the years a total of about 480 of these were put into service. With their twin headlamps and recessed windscreen they have a definite family resemblance to the buses and trolleybuses of the same period.

A later and more advanced design features an automatic control system to give fast acceleration to high speeds. This class is manufactured at the Riga Tramway Works, has an overall length of about 46 feet and can carry 160 passengers. The latest additions to the fleet are even more up-to-date and are imported from Czechoslovakia. They have a very strong affinity to the American PCC, with their sharply inclined windscreens and smooth lines; they have front and rear doors and are equipped with pantographs.

Some 30 or more years ago a visitor to Moscow observed: 'You can tell when the tram is full when one person is pushed in at the back and two fall out at the front'. If loads are still heavy – and it is one advantage of the tram that its capacity is high – changes have been made since then not only in the introduction of large modern bogie cars in place of small four-wheelers, but in the extension of the Metro on some of the busiest lines.

More recent practice in operating methods has included a seated conductor with a cash desk, as well as automatic doors to the platforms. A flat fare is paid for any distance, whereas the buses and trolleybuses have graded fares according to distance. This means that the trams are a very cheap mode of travel and are thus almost given the stigma of a 'class distinction', although their functions are rather different from those of the other forms of transport.

The tracks are laid to a gauge of 5 feet, the standard railway gauge in Russia. The livery is red and yellow, and either bow collectors or pantographs are used. At the beginning of 1963 there were forty different routes with a track length of about 260 miles. By comparison there were also 48 trolleybus routes with a mileage of 334. In one year all the public transport services in Moscow – including trams, buses, trolleybuses, and underground railways – carry some 3,600 million passengers.

For the future there are indications that certain tramway routes may be superseded as the underground spreads even further, but on the other hand new extensions have recently been made or are planned and any idea of abandoning the network altogether can only be seen as the most long-term objective. In the nearer prospect the intriguing suggestion has been promulgated that within a few years all fares will be abolished and public transport services will be free.

Tramways are widely used in the Soviet Union, a number of completely new systems having been brought into operation since the war. In 1936, 76 towns were operating this form of transport, with a total route mileage of nearly 3,900. There were then 9,800 cars and they carried more than 5,400 million passengers in the year. In 1963 trams were running in more than 100 towns and cities and they were carrying about 35 per cent of the total number of urban passengers.

XV

On Top to Ramleh
(Alexandria)

ONE of the most incongruous sights in Egypt must be a double-deck tram gliding past the streets of Alexandria. And as if to emphasise the incongruity, the double-decker does not run alone but is coupled to a more conventional-looking single-decker, resulting in a strange combination that cannot be seen anywhere else in the world. Then to increase the confusion, some of the cars incorporate second-hand equipment that once formed part of London trams.

The unique line on which all this happens is the Alexandria and Ramleh Electric Railway. Although it uses tramway-type cars with overhead wire and trolley poles, it is not a street tramway; it is laid on its own right of way adjacent to streets, although fenced off from them, and there are many road crossings where it traverses the suburbs of the city. The line starts at Place Zaghloul in Alexandria and runs a distance of about nine miles to a destination described as 'Victoria' in Ramleh; at two places along the route the line splits into two to serve different localities, but they soon converge again after each of these diversions.

Its origin can be traced back to 1869, when a horse tramway was constructed. Later on, steam was introduced as motive power, and eventually electric operation came in 1903.

The railway was built to serve an area along the Mediterranean coast eastward from Alexandria. This is now a densely-populated district with resorts and residences, and the line has a frequent service and carries heavy traffic.

Stops are fairly close together, so there is little opportunity for high speeds to be attained. Each stopping place has its own 'station', generally consisting of a platform and loading shelter. In places the line runs in a cutting or on a low embankment, but for most of its length it is alongside the roads and the houses that have been built nearby.

Place names *en route* make an agreeable diversion, as well as recalling both the location of the railway and the history of the country. Caesar's Camp and Cleopatra are natural enough, and equally indigenous are Sidi Gaber and Mustafa Pasha. Invoking the days of English domination are such names as Sporting Club, Chatby, Bulkeley and Fleming.

Destinations are shown on the indicators in both their English and their

Egyptian forms, so that the 'Victoria' which looks familiar to a Londoner appears side by side with an indecipherable squiggle that conveys the same information to an Egyptian. Unfortunately for the non-Egyptian 'spotter' the fleet numbers are also given in the native form, so that the compilation of a list requires the knowledge of an entirely unfamiliar set of symbols.

Much rebuilding of the rolling stock has taken place in recent years, with the result that the antique double-deckers – which had open balconies just like many of their British contemporaries – have given way to more modern all-enclosed vehicles. In view of the increased traffic, a number of single-deckers were given top decks. Nowadays the typical 'train' consists of a motored single-decker, which is for first-class passengers, coupled to a double-deck trailer which is for second-class passengers. All of them are long bogie cars, with entrances at each end.

Apart from the sight of the tall double-deckers, the Londoner may be made to feel at home by the fact that some of them run on trucks that once served in London. When the London tramways ceased in 1952, the massive equal-wheel bogies of the hill-climbing HR/2 class still had years of life left in them, and so they were shipped off to Alexandria. Here they were used to provide the motive power under new bodies that were built for the town trams in that city, but before long they were transferred to the Ramleh line, where the bodies were rebuilt to their present form.

The Londoner can also be reminded of home when he travels on the Alexandria town routes. These are now physically separated from the Ramleh line, although they are under the same management. Unlike the almost railway-like character of the interurban, these are more like conventional tramways.

Until not so many years ago, the town trams were extremely antiquated, including some with open ends that were doubtless popular enough in the hot sun of Egypt even if they were not in accord with the most modern practice. After the new bogie cars had been transferred to Ramleh, they had apparently left a taste for London equipment, for items from the London E/3 class were also imported and utilised in the construction of new four-wheelers. These are quite smart-looking vehicles running in pairs. As on the Ramleh line, the town services also have class distinction, but this time the motor car is relegated to providing second class while the trailer offers the relative luxury of first class.

Like their Ramleh counterparts, the town cars carry their fleet numbers in Egyptian characters, but fortunately they also carry them in Roman numerals as well, thus making the 'spotter's' job easier. It seems too that even the Egyptians have difficulty in deciphering the strange characters that pass for destinations, and in view of the large extent of illiteracy among their passengers, the undertaking makes things simple by using a colour code. This takes the form of different shaped symbols – including stars, triangles and diamonds – displayed on the front of the car to indicate the route it is following.

The 'main line' of some five miles in length extends from east to west across the town, from Nouzha to Mex, while other routes serve the harbour areas, but certain changes have involved the withdrawal of trams from a number of streets.

Karachi's diesel-powered trams. The engine is situated beneath the centre seats, and the flap giving
access to the radiator filler can be seen in the upper picture. *(T. M. Russell*

PLATE 23

An older type of Calcutta tram working on one of the routes in Howrah. Note the wire mesh to protect the driver.

(Hugh Ballment

On a spacious part of the Calcutta tramway system. The reserved tracks in the Maidan alongside Chowringhee Road.

(Hugh Ballmont

A Calcutta articulated tram at the busy Esplanade Junction.

(Hugh Ballment

PLATE 24

Once a common sight in Britain, lines of double-deck trams in the street are now only to be seen in Hong Kong. This is Des Voeux Road, in the city of Victoria on Hong Kong Island.

(Hong Kong Government

PLATE 25

Upper—a double-deck tram in Hong Kong.
Lower—the Peak Tramway in Hong Kong.

(R. Forty

(Hong Kong Government

PLATE 26

XVI

Diesels to Saddar
(Karachi)

THERE is something strange about the Karachi trams, although at first sight you may not realise precisely what it is. Poles and overhead wires seem the natural accompaniment to a tramway, so it may be a little time before you notice their absence here. And instead of the hum of electric motors, there is a noise like that of a bus, while in place of sparks from the trolley there is smoke from the exhaust. For the trams in Pakistan's capital city are not electrically operated – they are powered by diesel engines.

In appearance the cars themselves are light and almost flimsy. They are single-deckers with open sides and ends, an airy arrangement well suited to the hot climate. Seating is arranged in five sets of back-to-back benches across the width of the vehicle, giving a total capacity of 50 passengers. The seats are of wood, but they have padded backs, while the seats at the end just behind the driver are 'ladies only'. Additional luxury takes the form of shutters that can be let down to keep out some of the rain in bad weather. The conductor carries out his task of collecting fares by clambering along a footboard that runs the length of each side.

Each car is mounted on four wheels set at a wheelbase of 8 feet, and is 28 feet long. It is driven by a Perkins diesel engine that is mounted beneath the centre seat, the drive being by gearbox and chain to one of the axles. The controls consist of a throttle key, a gear lever and a clutch pedal, as well as a gong pedal, and these form part of the terminal ritual, for they have to be transferred by the driver from one end of the car to the other when it reverses at the terminus. In addition, there is a crank handle at each end, to work the hand brake which is the only form of braking employed.

Another item of operating ritual may also be seen at the terminus, when a man approaches with a water can. He lifts a flap beneath the centre seat at the side of the car and fills the radiator.

In spite of their non-electric motive power, the cars have electric lighting. They also have a fair turn of speed and are able to reach 20 or 25 miles an hour. The fleet numbers some 60 vehicles.

They are shedded in a depot in Bunder Road, and this too is unlike the normal tram depot in that it has facilities for maintaining internal combustion engines rather than electric motors. Another surprise is to see the fuel pumps, which are reminiscent of the petrol pumps of a motor filling station.

The two focal points of the system are Boulton Market in the west and Saddar in the east. These are joined by the 'main line' which follows the broad thoroughfare of Bunder Road. At the Boulton Market terminus, the tracks are laid in to the side of the wide road so that passengers may board at the kerb, while there is also a third line in the centre for through cars to Keamari if required. This is a busy point, where crowds board and alight while itinerant vendors press their wares on travellers. From here routes also run along Napier Road to Chakiwara and along Lawrence Road to Gandhi Gardens.

From the other centre at Saddar, two routes go off roughly at right angles to the 'main line' to reach Soldier Bazar in the north and Cantonment Station in the south. This latter route includes a section of roadside reserved track for about a mile along Frere Street, and this is where high speeds may be attained, accompanied by clouds of dust.

There is, in addition, the original route that extends beyond Boulton Market southwards for almost three miles dead straight to reach the wharves at Keamari. On this line the service is operated at peak hours when dockers require transport, and a driver at Boulton Market may suddenly find himself instructed by the inspector to take his charge through to Keamari.

The undertaking can trace its origin as far back as 1884, when the East India Tramways Company was formed with British capital. In the following year, due ceremony saw the inauguration of the line along Bunder Road to Keamari, together with branches intended for freight traffic. At first, motive power was supplied by steam locomotives, but these were soon given up and horses were employed instead.

Then in 1910 came the new mode of traction, when two petrol-engined cars were placed in service. Built in England in 1909, these were probably the first such vehicles to operate on a street tramway anywhere in the world. They were spindly-looking machines, with awnings supported on thin rails and with curtains at the sides, while the seats were of the cross-bench type for 46 passengers. Fuel consumption amounted to eight miles to the gallon.

Such was their success that by 1912 petrol engines had completely displaced the horses, and motor trams have been used ever since. The present fleet has been built up over the years, and is now equipped with diesel engines rather than petrol engines, resulting in improved performance.

In total the system amounts to ten miles of route, laid to a gauge of 4 feet, and it is the only tramway undertaking in the whole of Pakistan. The East India Tramways Company gave way in 1949 to the equally-exotically named Mohamedali Tramways Company.

XVII

Over The Hooghli
(Calcutta)

WHERE else have tram drivers had to be protected by wire netting?
Calcutta's trams have at times been the innocent objects of political
demonstrators, so stout screens had to be installed to protect the drivers
from flying stones or other missiles that might inadvertently come their way.
However, this is a rare occupational hazard, and normally the trams can go
peacefully about their task of transporting over one million passengers every day.

Conditions in this crowded Indian city have ensured the retention of
trams as the main form of transport. With its neighbour Howrah across the
Hooghli River, Calcutta has a population exceeding four millions and is a
principal port. Once described as a 'city of palaces and slums', it is densely
populated with poor working classes who need the cheapest mode of transport
to get them to and from their work.

Since there is no adequate network of local railways, the main burden
of this job falls on the tramways. In congested streets the need is for vehicles
carrying the largest possible number of passengers in the smallest amount
of road space. That means cramming them in, but since they demand cheap-
ness rather than luxurious travel, they are willing to accept the crush, just
as their opposite numbers in London are willing to accept the crush of the
Underground railways. In the circumstances only the tram is able to meet
the need.

Here is what one official of the transport undertaking says about his
charges:

'The tramways in Calcutta are an example that proves that trams are
by no means an outdated mode of transport even in modern times. Besides
being cheap, having great carrying capacity, being comparatively fast,
comfortable, reliable and regular, they form the nucleus of Calcutta's transport system and are a real part of the life of this great Eastern city'.

What are these trams like? Typical of the fleet is the long articulated
single-decker. Although two bodies share the intermediate bogie, to all
intents and purposes they are two separate cars, although of course they
move as one and are therefore more economical of road space. Unlike the
common run of articulated tram elsewhere, they have no central gangway
connecting the two sections of the unit. But, like the usual 'artic', they are
single ended, as all termini are provided with turning facilities.

Each half of the articulated car has an entrance at the centre and there is a class distinction between the two halves that is strange to British eyes.

The leading part is first class; it contains between 30 and 35 upholstered seats and it has the added luxury of electric fans that are much appreciated in the sticky heat, especially when it is crowded. The rear part of this two-in-one vehicle is for second-class passengers and is accordingly less luxurious and is without the fans; it contains seats for about 40 passengers.

However, as on many other undertakings, the seating capacity does not tell the whole story. As well as the 70 or so seats in the unit, it can also carry 100 or more standing, giving it a total capacity of as many as 200 in all and obviously making it a useful means of moving the crowds.

These articulated cars have been developed over a period of some 30 years. Up to the early 1930s the typical unit consisted of a four-wheel motor tram with a similar four-wheeler as a trailer. Then, when modernisation was decided on, the articulated bogie car was designed, along with bogie single units for the less heavily trafficked routes. In the half-dozen years up to 1939 about 180 new trams were put into commission to replace small four-wheelers. In 1939 came a streamlined version, distinguished by its curved ends and sleek lines.

Nowadays the fleet consists of some 450 cars which operate over about 40 miles of routes.

What are these routes like? One valuable feature is that many of them include long sections of reserved tracks, with the lines laid not in the carriage-way but at the side or in the central strip. Being thus removed from other traffic, the trams are able to obtain an uninterrupted right of way and to move as swiftly as possible. To this extent they do something to make up for the lack of full-scale railways.

This kind of layout can be seen, for example, in the famous thoroughfare of Chowringhee, one of Calcutta's finest streets. Here for a distance of about two miles the tracks run on a reservation at the side of the road, while grass and overhanging trees add to the pleasantness of the scene.

By this route, which is the busiest on the network with at peak times a car about every minute, passengers are brought as rapidly as they can be almost into the very heart of the city. In all about one-fifth of the whole system is laid on reservation.

One of the most impressive points on the network is Esplanade Junction, where there are two turning loops with trams seeming to go round and round like a perpetual merry-go-round. Spreading out into the suburbs the routes extend to such exotic sounding places as Tollyganj, Ballyganj, Kidderpore and Dumdum, as well as to the idyllic Eden Gardens.

The operator, the Calcutta Tramways Company, is a British concern which began working horse trams in 1881. By the turn of the century some 13 million passengers a year were being handled in 180 cars. Electrification came in 1902, and in the years that followed numerous extensions were made to meet the needs of the extensive suburbs.

In 1951 the company signed an agreement with the West Bengal Government under which its tenure was extended for 21 years until 1972. At the end of that time the Government will be able to acquire the company if it wants to.

One of the sights of the city, and one of the finest engineering features in India, is the bridge across the swirling waters of the great Hooghli river. Trams glide across this from Calcutta to reach the town of Howrah on the west bank of the river.

In Howrah itself there are other routes which were formerly quite unconnected with the main system although they were – and still are – operated by the same company. These lines were laid between 1905 and 1908, but the bridge that existed at that time was unable to accommodate such loads as trams.

This situation was not resolved until the present bridge was constructed, when the tracks were laid across at the same time. When this was done in 1943, trams could proceed across the bridge and provide through services between the two hitherto separate parts of the undertaking.

One last glance reveals one colourful but practical touch. In view of the high rate of illiteracy among the inhabitants, trams carry codes of different coloured shapes to indicate the routes on which they are travelling. This code takes the form of symbols on boards during the day, while at night the motor cars have similar illuminated signs.

XVIII

Double-Deckers in Victoria
(Hong Kong)

IT comes as something of a shock to the English traveller to discover that the streets of the mystic East are swarming with double-deck trams that would not have looked out of place in Sheffield or Stockport. That is the case in the British colony of Hong Kong, where trams serve Victoria, the principal city of Hong Kong Island.

Perhaps the presence of double-deckers is not so strange when it is remembered that they were built and operated by a British company, who seem to have had memories of their homeland when they installed their lines in this corner of Asia almost within the shadow of the Chinese mainland.

But a little closer look will reveal that these dark-green trams are rather different from those of Britain. True, they are double-deck four-wheelers, high and somewhat angular, with the central headlamp and the trolley pole once familiar at home. But an examination of them reveals important differences.

To begin with, there are two entrances. One is at the front, next to the driver, while the other is at the back in the conventional position. The front entrance leads directly to the single stairway that gives access to the upper deck, while the rear entrance leads only to the lower deck.

Now comes another contrast, for the two decks are of different classes. The upper is for first-class passengers, while the lower is for second-class. Such a division of classes, while common on railways, appears strange to British eyes at first, for it was a feature that was almost unknown on British tramways; although Liverpool once operated 'first class only' cars, there was rarely any formal class distinction on street tramcars in Britain. Moreover, in Hong Kong this class differentiation is reflected in the fares, for it is cheaper to travel downstairs.

The upper deck is fitted with transverse wooden seats, to accommodate two passengers on one side of the gangway and only one on the other side; the lower deck has longitudinal wooden seats and also allows room for a number of standing passengers, for the cheaper accommodation is naturally patronised by the poorer class of traveller.

A further difference from customary British practice will also be noted, in that there is only one staircase. This is because the vehicle is single-ended, as there is a turning loop at each terminus.

The fleet is largely of modern design and origin, for in the years since 1950 the operator – the Hong Kong Tramways Company – has undertaken an extensive programme of reconstruction which has entailed the building of many new trams to augment the stock. The bodies are designed by the company and are built locally, both by the company itself and by local dockyards. Constructed on a steel underframe with steel bulkheads, the new bodies have framing of teak and panelling of aluminium. Air-operated folding doors are fitted, as well as carbon-insert trolley heads.

Tramways started in Hong Kong in 1904 with a fleet of only 26. Since then traffic has grown enormously and the fleet has increased accordingly. By 1953 there were over 120, while this has now gone up to some 150. The rise in traffic in recent years can be seen by the fact that while in 1949 some 109 million passengers were carried, by 1963 the corresponding figure was over 190 million. The population of this crowded island has been expanding rapidly, and the tramways have had their share of this reflected in their traffic receipts.

Heavier loadings have also called for improvements in the track, of which the company has about 19 miles, all on the gauge of 3 ft. 6 in. One example of this improvement was in the eastern part of the system, on the road between King's Road and Causeway Bay, where the tracks were re-aligned and provided with new foundations, while elsewhere loading islands have been installed for the benefit of passengers boarding in the bustling streets.

The tramways' territory is the city of Victoria, much of which is built on reclaimed land on the coast, huddling in the shadow of the mountains that make up much of the island.

This sprawling city is the chief business centre of the colony, and the main streets are lined with imposing blocks of offices and banks representing the vast trade carried on in the port. There are high modern buildings along the streets, with hotels to cater for the tourist trade which is another activity of the island, while on the other side is the waterfront overlooking one of the finest natural harbours, with ships from all over the world.

The double-track main line extends right across Victoria from Kennedy Town in the west to Shaukiwan in the east. There are intermediate turning loops at Whitty Street, Western Market and North Point, for the main line is worked – in conjunction with the branch to the Race Course at the pleasantly-named Happy Valley – as three overlapping services.

The longest service runs from Shaukiwan to Western Market, a distance of more than $6\frac{1}{2}$ miles. The other two services – between North Point and Whitty Street and between Happy Valley and Kennedy Town – are each almost five miles in length. Journey time is between 35 and 40 minutes, and the traffic is sufficient to call for a two or three minute headway on each.

At busy times in the heart of the city there is a car about every half minute, so that in such principal thoroughfares as Des Voeux Road there is a constant stream practically nose to tail on each track. This is now the only city in the world where it is possible to see lines of double-deck trams, once such a common sight in the streets of Britain. A glimpse of the contrasts of the East is observed when the trams mingle with one of the few rickshaws that still remain as reminders of a past mode of conveyance.

Fares are cheap, as indeed prices and wages generally are in the colony. There is a flat fare for any distance. This is 20 cents (the equivalent of 3d.) for first-class travel on the upper deck, and only 10 cents (a mere 1½d.) for second class on the lower deck.

The maximum distance for which you can travel for this fare is over 6½ miles – at the second-class fare this works out at the incredibly low rate of less than ½d. per mile! In addition there are monthly tickets and concessionary fares, amounting in all to the fact that the tramways provide mass transport at the lowest possible rates.

Apart from the trams in the streets, there is another tramway in Hong Kong. This is the Peak Tramway, which is in fact a funicular railway. It climbs up from the centre of Victoria to the Peak, the mountain that rises steeply behind the city. The upper terminus of the line is some 1,300 feet above sea level and the maximum gradient is an impressive 1 in 2.

The Peak Tramway was built in 1888 in order to make development possible in this hitherto inaccessible district above the crowded city. Until 1924, when a motor road was built, it was the only means of transport to this area. Now it carries nearly two million passengers a year in its modern streamlined cars, each of which has a capacity of 62.

The line is deservedly popular with tourists and takes a merited place on the itinerary of the visitor. As the car rises from the lower level, there are wonderful views of the expanse of the harbour as well as of Kowloon on the mainland and of the neighbouring islands. Only ten minutes is occupied in making the climb, and for those ascending for the first time it passes too quickly. The first-class single fare for the journey is 60 cents.

These four photographs indicate the variety of the rolling stock on the Tokyo tramways. American influence on design is obvious.

(*J. W. Higgins; R. Forty*)

PLATE 27

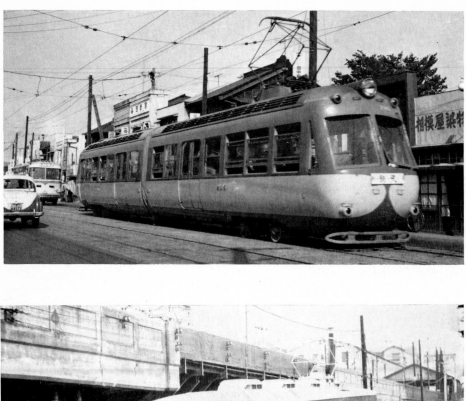

Scenes on the T.K.K., the suburban tramways of Tokyo. The upper picture shows one of the distinctive 'caterpillar' articulated cars. The destination on the indicator of the car in the lower picture is intriguing to Western eyes.

(J. W. Higgins)

PLATE 28

XIX

Crowds and Catastrophes
(Tokyo)

TOKYO's trams have survived the ordeals of both natural and man-made catastrophes. Fire has often ravaged areas of the city's old wooden buildings, while the earthquakes that periodically hit Japan have caused widespread destruction. In the great earthquake of 1923, for example, well over 700 trams were destroyed. During the Second World War about 600 were lost. In each case the system has sprung up again from the ruins.

The trams have also up to now survived other changes that have taken place, although they appear to be seriously threatened by them. Large-scale rebuilding after the 1923 earthquake changed the pattern of the city as new areas were developed away from the old ravaged districts. These new areas are outside the range of the tramways, which have not been extended to serve them; instead they have been served by underground and suburban electric railways which now form the most important means of public transport in Tokyo.

Today therefore the trams provide local transport over short distances rather than into the extensive suburbs. They take second place to the railways, which with the growth of new lines reaching into the tramway territory in the centre, may threaten their very existence.

They may also be threatened by the increasing congestion in the streets, a common situation as road traffic grows in intensity. The trams are helped, though, by being provided at busy points with 'stations' – some with subways to the pavement – so that passengers do not have to brave the dangers of the traffic.

In spite of the construction of highways and viaducts for motor traffic the time may come when the only palliative left may be to segregate public transport from the streets altogether by the construction of underground railways, which would in their turn replace the surface tramways.

Nevertheless it would be a mistake to underrate the importance of the present-day system. Even today there are some 1,100 cars working on about 40 different routes. Moreover the density of the traffic has put a heavy load on them, for as each new railway has come along it has brought in more and more people to be distributed in the central districts.

It was in 1882 that trams began to operate in Tokyo during the period when Japan became open to outside influence after centuries of isolation from the world. Eventually there were three separate companies, but there was little co-ordination and services were unsatisfactory. At last the three were unified, but even this did not have the desired effect, so in 1911 the whole undertaking was acquired by the city authorities who have worked it ever since.

A drastic modernisation programme was carried through during the 1930s. This largely followed American practice, with the result that the cars of this period (and indeed those of the later period) show a definite American influence. In 1936 a fleet of some 1,700 was operating over a mileage of approximately 285.

An unusual feature of the electric lines was the use of two trolley poles in the same manner as a trolleybus. A tram normally requires only the positive overhead wire and one pole, as the negative return is made via the running rails. But in certain circumstances where it was desirable to avoid having the return circuit travel by way of the rails, or where such a return was unreliable, the second wire was used with a second trolley pole.

Such a double-trolley method was at one time employed on one route in London. Here it was intended to obviate wandering currents that might have interfered with the sensitive instruments of the nearby Greenwich observatory. The double trolley was also the practice in Cincinatti and Havana. In Tokyo it was generally replaced by the normal single pole after the 1945 war, although on some lines it was still to be seen as late as 1953.

After the war much effort had to be put into getting the system into working order again. By 1951 as many as 142 miles of line had been brought back into use, compared with the total of 280 in pre-war days. By this time some 780 cars were in operation carrying well over a million passengers a day.

By 1961 there were over 1,100 in the fleet, carrying as many as 1.7 million passengers every day. Although one new route was constructed between 1950 and 1956, the total route mileage during this decade declined slightly to 133, making it obvious that loads were on the increase.

During this period a number of new trams were built. In 1955, for example, over 50 additions were made to the fleet.

A few of these newcomers were allegedly 'PCC's' although they showed little resemblance to their supposed American forebears. The latest type are of lightweight construction and built for a comparatively short life, in view of the possible disappearance of the tramways in future years. All cars are bogie single-deckers, operating singly, and all have bow collectors except the few 'PCC's' which are graced with pantographs.

As to the interior, the British visitor is likely to be struck by its bareness. In effect it is a vast echoing hall with austere seats arranged lengthwise around the edges. The seats are sufficient for only about 20 people; the rest have to stand. And the 'rest' is usually a large number, for that is the purpose behind this bare interior – passengers are just crammed in until they are packed solid. Standing capacity of each vehicle is officially put at about 70, but unofficially it is held to be a good deal more.

The adoption of longitudinal seating on this plan is found all over Japan, not only on trams but on railway trains as well. It makes the most efficient use of space, even if the standard of comfort is not high.

Externally the Tokyo trams are kept in good condition in their present smart livery of buff with a red band. The traffic rule of left-hand running may give them superficially something of a familiar look, but this is soon dispelled by a glance at the destination indicator which has a decorative array of Japanese characters that convey nothing whatever to the average westerner.

One oddity in the network was route 14 which was of narrow gauge – against the 4 ft. 6 in. gauge of the rest of the system. This one line was physically isolated and had its own fleet of some 30 cars which have now been rebuilt to standard gauge. This is so far the only casualty resulting from the intensive building of underground railways.

Another oddity of more recent origin is a monorail, brought into use for the 1964 Olympic Games to link the city with the airport. But it appears that this form of transport is unlikely to be widely adopted for commuter traffic, and new underground railway construction is going ahead. Apart from the trams and railways, transport in Tokyo is also provided by motor buses as well as by a limited number of trolleybuses which were first introduced in 1952.

The continuing importance of the tramways is indicated by a few figures. The number of passengers they carried amounted to 442 million in 1948; in 1953 this had risen to 598 million, while in 1954 it reached 619 million. By 1959 this had fallen slightly but still recorded an impressive 592 million.

There is another tramway in the Tokyo area, but this has no connection with the city network and is operated by a separate undertaking, the Tokyo Electric Express Railway. This concern owns railways, among other things, but it also possesses three tram routes in the west and south-west of Tokyo. These meet the city lines in the suburb of Shibuya and then fan out to form basically a main line with two branches.

Total route mileage of this concern is only about ten, but it is sufficiently busy to require a fleet of 70, including four new ones put into service as recently as 1964. In spite of duplication by an underground railway in the course of construction, the trams seem likely to remain. Although parts of the routes are laid in the streets, much consists of reserved track.

Most of the cars again are large bogie single-deckers not unlike their city counterparts, but the most distinctive in appearance are the 'caterpillars'. These are articulated vehicles running on five axles; two bogies support the outer ends, but the centre is carried on one single pair of wheels. The green livery, together with the curved ends and inswept lower parts of the bodies, justify the nickname given to these streamliners.

XX

Camberwell to Brighton
(Melbourne)

MELBOURNE has been called the most English city in Australia, and the trams both confirm and refute this title. Whereas its more American-ised rival Sydney has dispensed with trams and tended to favour motorways on the American style, Melbourne has retained its trams as the main form of public transport. But they are quite different from the traditional British pattern.

Look at the typical Melbourne tram. Take the SW6 class as an example; the first of the type was introduced in 1939 and many others of the same basic design have been built since. It is a massive bogie single-decker, over 46 feet long, weighing nearly 17 tons, and powered by four 40 horse-power motors.

It is of the 'drop centre' type that is characteristically Australian, having been developed in Melbourne and used extensively not only there but in Sydney, Brisbane, Adelaide and Launceston. The outstanding feature of this design is that the centre part between the bogies is slightly lower than the end portions and contains the two entrances with large space for standing passengers in the central 'well'.

The SW6 has sliding doors, and seats either 48 or 52 passengers. Up-holstered seats are provided in the two saloons at either end, although those in the 'well' are of wood. The motorman has a separate compartment at each end, entered from an outside door. Other members of the fleet are of a generally similar pattern, some having resilient wheels for quiet running.

The significance of this design is its high overload capacity. Apart from the 50 or so seated passengers, there is claimed to be room for about another 100 standing, so it obviously has an advantage over the motor bus of more limited capacity.

Some comparison can be made here between the British bus with its restricted standing, and the London underground railways with their great load-carrying ability. Passengers are prepared to travel standing rather than to stand waiting at the stop until they can get a seat in a bus.

This then is a clue to the continuance of tramway operation in Melbourne, as it is in so many other cities. It also points to the reason why in recent years certain bus routes have been replaced by tramways.

Take Bourke Street for example. Until 1940 this was a cable tramway, but then buses were put on instead. Not only did they prove less satisfactory than their predecessors in maintaining the service, but people expressed a preference for trams, for the double-deck bus has never been widely popular in Australia; thus after a number of years of unsatisfactory working, during which time the buses had perforce to remain since materials for construction were not obtainable, it was decided to go ahead and lay in a completely new tramway.

The Bourke Street route was opened in 1955. It involved about six miles of new tracks to provide a route running from Spencer Street in the city, along Bourke Street and through Northcote to East Preston.

When the changeover took place a reporter on the *Melbourne Argus* said: 'Traffic never flowed more smoothly in Melbourne's infamous rush hour that it did in this new tram street yesterday. Being a veteran of five bumpy years' experience on the double-deck buses, I can vouch for the improved comfort of the trams. There's no ear-piercing scream of brakes, no sudden lurching stops, no jumping for safety as the bus swings to the kerb.'

In 1956 trams made a comeback on another route which had been worked by buses after the cessation of the cable cars. This was to East Brunswick via Nicholson Street.

A glance at the finances of the time reveals the prominence of the trams and the economics which prompted their favour. In the year 1952–53 they showed a surplus of some £24,000 while the buses had a loss of over £103,000. Although they were more expensive to operate, their receipts were higher: over 55d. per mile against only 44d. per mile on the buses. Their ascendancy was clearly indicated by the fact that in that same year they carried as many as 207 million passengers while the buses carried only 61 million.

The layout of the city has also favoured tramway operation. The nineteenth-century planners were far-sighted enough to design their city on spacious lines, with a grid of wide straight streets, some of them nearly 100 feet in width. There is therefore plenty of room for tracks down the centre of the thoroughfare.

In addition the grid-iron layout results in a series of parallel streets – such as Flinders Street, Collins Street and Bourke Street – which help to divide the traffic flow. There are also equally spacious suburban roads, such as St. Kilda Road, which are amply wide enough to carry the tracks without obstructing the stream of traffic. And these broad highways make it possible to employ the large bogie cars that are of a size commensurate with them.

The visitor from England is likely to feel himself at home among the names in Melbourne. He can find Richmond, Kew and Camberwell, Box Hill and Malvern, Preston and Foots Cray as well as Brighton, suburbs which recall the establishment by English settlers. He can also discover a real Brighton Beach, while the trams will take him from the city centre to the beaches in the south in little more than ten minutes.

Melbourne, the capital of the state of Victoria, today has a population of about 1½ million. Transport is provided by the Melbourne and Metropolitan Tramways Board, which operates some 750 trams, as well as buses, in the city and its suburbs.

In earlier days Melbourne went in for cable traction in a big way. During their heyday almost 600 'trains' were running over some 45 miles of route. The first line was opened in 1885 along Flinders Street to Richmond, and others followed along Collins Street, Bourke Street, Elizabeth Street and Swanston Street.

Melbourne's cable cars were different from those in San Francisco and certain other towns. Instead of a single vehicle, they consisted of a two-car unit comprising a grip car, or 'dummy', hauling a trailer. The dummy was a peculiar-looking contrivance; it had a low floor reaching almost to road level, and it had open sides and ends with a roof supported on posts.

Along the length of this vehicle passengers sat on two longitudinal seats back to back and facing outwards, while at the ends more seats faced forward and backward. The front seats gave the passenger a clear and unobstructed view forward; perhaps too much so, for there was nothing between him and the rapidly advancing world except a flimsy-looking mesh fence. In the middle of this vehicle the gripman stood manipulating his controls. Coupled to the grip car was a more conventional type of open-ended saloon trailer.

The cable cars had a remarkably long life. Although some went in the 1920s, others persisted well into the 1930s and it was not until 1940 that the last of them ceased work.

The extent of the cable network influenced the comparatively late arrival of electric traction. Although an electric tramway – the first in Australia – began operation in 1889 on the outskirts of the city between Box Hill and Doncaster, it lasted only a few years and it was not until the second decade of the twentieth century that electric tramways got under way in Melbourne itself.

When they did come they were constructed by several different undertakings, but in 1919 the Melbourne and Metropolitan Tramways Board was formed to take them over.

The Board carried out large-scale development which involved the replacement of cable tramways by electric, the construction of new lines and the introduction of more modern rolling stock. In the years between 1922 and 1946 the Board put into service 750 new cars and built 29 miles of lines, including reserved track sections in the suburbs to such points as West Coburg and Essendon Aerodrome.

An interesting example of development took place to the west of the city in Foots Cray and Maribyrnong. During the 1939–45 war, factories were built in the Maribyrnong area, a district that before that time had been described as 'famous mostly for dog coursing, lack of population and general inaccessibility'. Now with transport needed to serve the factories, the tramways were extended, largely on reserved tracks and including a private bridge over the river.

This brought the line gradually nearer to the Foots Cray system, which consisted of three short routes physically isolated from the rest of the network. For many years there had been talk of linking Foots Cray with the main system by a direct route across reclaimed land, but eventually in 1954 a reserved track extension was made to link them with the Maribyrnong line, enabling a through service to the city to be started. In 1962, though, the local routes in Foots Cray were abandoned, mainly because, with sharp curves and limited clearances, they had had to use small four-wheelers rather than the large bogies of the main system.

Two other abandoned routes are worthy of mention. These were both operated by the Victorian Railways. In 1906 the line from St. Kilda to Brighton was opened; this was unusually of the 5 ft. 3 in. gauge as opposed to the standard 4 ft. 8½ in. of the rest of Melbourne's tramways. The second railway-owned tramway, from Sandringham to Black Rock, was opened in 1919 on the standard gauge. Both lines used cars of the characteristic drop-centre type.

XXI

Symbol of a City
(San Francisco)

LOOK at any 'Come to America' advertisement and the chances are
that it depicts a San Francisco cable car. If England is traditionally
the land of thatched cottages, then the United States is the land of the
cable car. Both views may be equally misleading, but to the whole world
these little trams are the symbol of the city of San Francisco.

That is why they couldn't scrap them. They wanted to get rid of these
old-timers that scrambled up and down the steep hills, but they had reckoned
without the hold that this historic form of transport had taken on the popular
mind.

No sooner had the authorities said they were to go than a 'Save the Cable
Cars Committee' was set up and battle commenced. Public indignation was
strong; even in this land of modernity the citizens had a soft spot for this
reminder of a past age. San Francisco also had electric trams, trolleybuses
and motor buses, but none of these had the same appeal.

The result of the struggle was that the cable cars were saved. And they
look like going on for ever.

It is appropriate that they should remain as a national monument here,
for San Francisco claims to be the first home of the cable car. Its invention
is attributed to Andrew Hallidie, a Londoner of Scottish origin who settled
in America.

He was obviously a humanitarian as well as an inventor, for he was shocked
at the hard life of the horses that had to work in the San Francisco of the
1870s. The city is surrounded by steep hills, and the animals had an arduous
task in getting the heavy trams up the inclines. Moreover the built-up area
was spreading, so that transport would be called for on gradients that even
the most hard-working horses could not cope with.

To meet these conditions Hallidie suggested the use of a cable tramway.
The principle of it was that an endless moving cable ran in a channel between
the rails; each car was fitted with a gripper which could grab hold of the
cable and impart its motion to the vehicle. Stopping was accomplished by
disengaging the gripper. The cable was driven from a central power house,
where it went around a great pulley. By this means, no matter what the
gradient the cars could move safely at a constant speed.

Many were sceptical of the idea at first, but he succeeded in obtaining

Above – two types of Melbourne tram, showing the entrances and the 'drop centre'. The car in the second photograph has modernised ends and is fitted with PCC-type equipment.

Left – a reminder of cable car days in Melbourne. A cable tram 'dummy' finds a last resting place.

(K. J. Walker

PLATE 29

Trams in Melbourne's wide streets; a view of Princes Bridge over the River Yarra.

The typical 'drop centre' variety of Melbourne tram.

PLATE 30

San Francisco's cable cars glide up and down the city's steep hills. Here a car is being turned on the turntable at the Powell Street terminus. *(U.S. Information Service*

PLATE 31

Left – a cable car on San Francisco's Powell Street and Hyde Street route.

Below – a typical American 'trolley car' of an earlier generation makes a 'fan trip' on the Municipal Railway of San Francisco.
(Thomas C. Swinney

Gothenberg's conception of a four-track junction on a suburban tram route.   *(F. van Dam*

PLATE 32

powers to build his first cable tramway on the steep Clay Street hill. Work started in 1872 and the line was to be ready in the following year.

Unless it was complete by 1st August, 1873, Hallidie forfeited the authorisation he had obtained from the authorities. It was a frantic rush to get everything finished in time but on the vital morning all was ready for the trial run.

No one was quite sure that it would work, and many expected to see the little car go speeding down the hill and be dashed to pieces at the bottom. Hallidie himself was apparently the only person who seemed confident of the outcome. So much so that instead of starting the first journey from the bottom of the hill as any more cautious person would have done, he decided to start from the top. This was too much for the man he had employed to operate the car; he took one look at his frail charge and the fearsome descent and then promptly went off home.

It was left to Hallidie himself to take the controls. He stepped aboard, engaged the gripper and the car made its first journey down the gradient. It worked, and a new era in city transport had opened. A month later and the cars began to carry passengers in public service.

The cable cars were a success. By 1890 San Francisco had 600 of them on ten routes. And the idea spread to other places; to Chicago, for example, which eventually had a vast network. And it even travelled overseas; the hilly Scottish city of Edinburgh built up a fleet of some 200 which lasted into the 1920s, while in Australia, Melbourne had an extensive system which did not entirely disappear until 1940.

In course of time, though, the cable cars began to fall before the newer electric cars to whom equally the gradients meant little, while they in turn were displaced by the pounding motor bus. In San Francisco the number of cable cars had dropped to less than 100 by 1937. But in 1947 a halt was called, and now the city has the only true cable tramways in the world.

The surviving system numbers about 30 cars operating on three routes. Two of the routes terminate at the junction of Powell Street and Market Street; they both run along Powell Street and then they divide, one going to Mason Street and the other to Hyde Street.

The third line runs east and west, at right angles to the other two, traversing California Street from a junction with Market Street to Van Ness Street. The Mason Street line is about 1½ miles in length, Hyde Street about 2 miles, and California Street about 1½ miles.

The cars are of two different types. California Street uses double-enders that simply reverse at the end of the route. But the Mason and Hyde routes use single-ended cars which are turned on turntables at each end of their journey.

One of the sights of the city is the turntable at the Market Street terminus of these Powell Street lines. This is a busy spot, enlivened by the manoeuvre of turning the car, an activity in which passengers delight to join while the cameras of tourists click merrily.

All the cars are single-deckers and are partly open and partly enclosed. The Mason and Hyde single-enders have an enclosed saloon at one end and an open-sided section at the other, while the California Street double-enders have a central saloon with an open section at each end.

In the open-sided part of the car the gripman can be seen at work with his levers. A massive lever controls the grip, imparting the movement of the cable to the car. The manipulation of this calls for considerable skill, for it is not simply a matter of using it for starting and stopping; there are curves and junctions to be negotiated, and these call for split-second timing to ensure that the cable is released at the right moment, otherwise it can get hopelessly entangled or jerked off the supporting pulleys.

The gripman also has the important task of braking the car. With the steep gradients involved – these may exceed an incline of 1 in 5 – efficient braking is obviously vital. In fact there is not one brake but several.

One of these is operated by the gripman with his foot; this applies a brake to the front wheels. The conductor can also work a similar brake on the rear wheels by means of a handle on the rear platform. Next there is a track brake, operated by the gripman with a lever; this applies a wood block to the rails near the rear wheels. There is also an emergency brake consisting of a wedge which can be jammed into the cable slot between the rails; this is a last resort only, since once it is applied it requires drastic measures to withdraw it.

The cable itself is powered from a central power house, which keeps it moving at a steady speed of nine miles an hour. The cable is made of steel, over an inch in diameter, and it normally lasts some six or eight months, after which time it has to be renewed. This is a costly business, and it is one of the factors making the system expensive to maintain. In all there are some ten miles of cables constantly rumbling along their channels beneath the rails in the streets.

Occasionally a cable breaks, and then the service comes to a halt until repairs are made. The repair gang have first to locate the break, which they do by inspection through the slot. When they have found both ends they make a temporary join, then the cable is set in motion again and kept moving slowly until the repaired section appears in the power house. Here a permanent join is made before normal service is resumed.

As well as being an attraction in themselves the cable cars allow the visitor to see some of the sights of the city. Take a journey and note the comments of the San Francisco Municipal Railway, the operator of the city's public transport. Sample the Mason and Hyde lines from the Powell Street terminus. These take you through Chinatown:

'A fascinating community in which reside more than 20,000 happy persons . . . exotic shops with the wares of old Cathay . . . mysterious alleys that lure the venturesome visitor.'

If you can ignore this lure you can continue on the Mason Street line over Nob Hill, traditional home of San Francisco's élite, and then on to the terminus for Fisherman's Wharf:

'Nets spread to dry and be repaired close to anchored fishing boats . . . marine grottoes whose sidewalk pitchmen invite you to partake of crustacean delicacies. . . .'

The Hyde Street line takes you to Aquatic Park, while the California Street line also serves Chinatown and goes through the financial district.

Guide books of earlier days, when the system was more extensive, recommended round tours by cable car. Here is one:

'We suggest that when you visit San Francisco, you make the following "Grand Tour": Starting at Union Square, walk down Powell one block to O'Farrell, and take a westbound red car. This will take you around the edge of Nob Hill and over Russian Hill to the Bay. Walk three blocks east to famous Fisherman's Wharf, then up Taylor to Bay (three blocks) and take the green and cream Powell cable through the Latin Quarter. At California Street change to the westbound red car and ride through the apartment house district, getting off at Steiner. Walk three blocks north and board the Washington-Jackson car, which will bring you to the edge of Chinatown, over Nob Hill and back to Union Square.'

The San Francisco Municipal Railway was formed in 1912, taking over formerly separate transport undertakings, although the California Street Railway Company (operator of the California Street cable cars) did not become part of the Municipal Railway until 1944. In 1961 the Municipal Railway operated some 500 buses, about 300 trolleybuses and 100 electric trams, apart from the cable cars.

Now, while the old form of transport is preserved, one of the most modern is being considered. This will take the shape of a rapid transit system that will provide fast travel on rails away from the car-infested highways.

XXII

Survivals and Revivals

TRAMS are noted for longevity, a characteristic which has meant that they often soldier on long after they might have been expected to retire. Moreover, in some places they seem to have been overlooked by time, so that where in the limelight of the big city they may have been abandoned or modernised, in the lesser-lit outposts they may linger on like ghosts of the past, neither dying nor fading away.

At the same time, they have occasionally been given a new lease of life. They have strangely been revived long after they have been given up as hopeless. This final section is a glance at a few of these survivals and revivals in odd corners of the world.

San Francisco is not the only place in the world that can boast of cable cars. Back in Britain, at the North Wales seaside resort of Llandudno, there are cable trams that come into operation every summer to climb the steep gradients up the local eminence of the Great Orme's Head.

Of course, it has to be admitted that the Great Orme Railway is not quite like the San Francisco Municipal Railway. The San Francisco cars have a continuously moving cable, and a gripman works the mechanism to connect and disconnect the cars with the cable. On the Great Orme, on the other hand, the trams are kept permanently connected to the cable, the movement of which is controlled from the engine house.

This difference helps to explain the operating peculiarities of the Great Orme. For one thing, it is in two halves; each is of single track with a passing loop midway. There is a cable for each half, and there are also two cars on each half, one going up while the other comes down so that they meet at the loop. At the half-way point, which is also the site of the winding station, passengers have to change cars to complete their journey.

Another peculiarity is that the cars are fitted with a trolley pole running on an overhead wire, as though they were electrically powered. However, this is not to pick up the current to drive them, it is to operate a signalling system; the wire connects a telephone on each car with the power station so that the driver can let the engineman know when all is ready and the cable can be started.

The two halves of the line are completely different in character. The lower half looks just like a conventional street tramway, for it is located in narrow roads in the town of Llandudno – one is so narrow that other traffic has to be prohibited when the line is in operation. Here are the steepest gradients, the most severe being a stiff 1 in 4.

The upper half is quite different, for this is away from the streets altogether. It is on private right of way across bleak open country, and as the track is not paved the cable can be seen gliding over its pulleys between the rails.

The Great Orme line is about a mile in total length and was opened in 1902 and 1903. The four cars in use are bogie single-deckers with open ends and seating 48 passengers. They date from the opening of the railway, which was formerly a separate company but has been owned by Llandudno Urban District Council since 1948.

France has swept away its trams almost as thoroughly as Britain, so that two of the survivors are all the more remarkable. Each of these two consists of only one route, while the total mileage of the two together is less than six. Moreover, in the one case the line was completely re-equipped with modern rolling stock, while in the other the route itself is quite out of the ordinary.

The modernised line is in the industrial town of St. Etienne. Here a whole fleet of thirty new trams was introduced in 1958 and 1959 to work one line which is less than four miles in length.

The cars are streamliners that look rather like the PCCs of Brussels, although they are narrower as they run on the metre gauge. They are 45 feet long and have seats for 22 passengers with room for nearly 90 standing.

A Mancunian may get a shock when he sees one of the destinations on the indicators, for one of the termini is Belle Vue. The other is Terrasse, and at each there is a turning loop. The route runs straight across the town and is of double track throughout.

The narrow streets and the heavy traffic are the reasons why this route was retained as the sole railed transport of the undertaking, which in addition operates several bus and trolleybus services. The route is so busy that at peak times there is a car every 1½ minutes, and the only way this heavy load can be squeezed through the congested thoroughfares of the town is by the use of trams which require minimum clearance on their fixed tracks.

The second French survivor is equally strange. This is in the great seaport of Marseilles, where there used to be an extensive system. In recent years, though, all the lines have been replaced by buses or trolleybuses – with one exception.

This odd one out is route 68, which is a mere two miles long. Apart from the fact that it makes a lone stand for railed traction in the otherwise railless streets of the town, its peculiarity is that one-quarter of its length is in tunnel.

The city end is an underground station. Leaving this to start their journey the trams pass through a half-mile-long subway beneath congested streets. Here they have a completely uninterrupted run free from other traffic so that the journey is swift and sure, an important factor in making this line a popular one. Indeed it is so heavily loaded that at peak times there is a car every two minutes.

The line comes up into daylight to emerge into the Boulevard Chave, which it traverses for some way before going on to a length of reserved track to reach the suburb of Saint Jean du Desert. It continues until it arrives at St. Pierre depot, where it turns around a loop to reach its own station, almost within the confines of the depot itself.

Originally the subway was the track of a steam-worked railway that was constructed in 1893. For twelve years its passengers had to endure the smoky tunnels before electrification came along and cleared the air. Now some twenty bogie trams rush along the line; they can trace their origin as far back as 1905, but they have been much rebuilt since to bring them up to more modern standards.

In far-off Australia the traveller can still find the only true 'interurban' that has existed on that continent. This is in Adelaide, the capital of South Australia. All the city's other tramways have been abandoned, the last of them ceasing in 1958, but this one interurban continues to operate.

Starting from the centre of Adelaide it extends a distance of just over six miles to the popular seaside resort of Glenelg. Once upon a time this too was a steam-worked railway, but as it traversed the street for some distance, it was not popular as such, hence after a good deal of negotiation it was decided to complete the job and convert it entirely into a tramway. It was accordingly taken over by the local transport authority, who in 1929 rebuilt it as a high-speed interurban tramway, converting it from 5 ft. 3 in. gauge to 4 ft. 8½ in. in the process.

The line now runs for about half a mile in the streets of Adelaide at one end, while the other end includes a similar distance in the streets of Glenelg. The rest of the route is on private right of way, double-track the entire distance and including such landmarks as a bridge over a 'real' railway and sidings at a racecourse.

Special rolling stock was provided when the metamorphosis took place. As befits an unusual line they are something special and are the biggest trams ever built in Australia. Thirty in number, they are over 56 feet long, weighing 23 tons and are able to seat 64 passengers as well as carry a large standing load. At busy times they can be coupled together in pairs, and can dash along at speeds up to 50 miles an hour to complete the journey in about twenty minutes.

Although the United States now has few tramways one of those few has the distinction of being 'international'. Way down in Texas is the city of El Paso, while facing it across the Rio Grande is Juarez in Mexico. Joining the two is a circular tram route, three miles round, which twice cuts across the international border. At these points there are the usual customs formalities, but different in this case by being carried out in a 'trolley car' with the officials making their inspection of the mixed bag of passengers of both nationalities.

The two 'halves' of the route are different in character, reflecting the two nations. From the typically American side the scenery changes as the border is crossed, where the Spanish architecture and language predominate. The cars themselves, though now having assumed something of a cosmopolitan nature, are definitely American by birth, having first seen the light of day in San Diego before coming to their present home. Some 15 of them circulate on this unique service.

One of the latest revivals is also in Texas and is perhaps the oddest of the lot. Imagine a tramway which simply carries passengers between a car park and a department store – and carries them entirely free! Of course, it is not disinterested, for the line was built by the proprietors of the store to make it easy for their customers to do their shopping.

It came about in this way. At one time the store ran a free bus service to bring its patrons in from the car park which was a little way from the shopping centre. But traffic congestion became so bad, and at busy times the number of buses that had to be used became so uneconomic, that the idea occurred to the owner of the store: why not build a tramway?

So that is what he did. And it is not a plain ordinary tramway in the street, either. After circling around the enormous car park, where there is room for as many as 3,000 private cars and where passengers board their free service at neatly-constructed stations, the line sweeps around a curve and disappears into a tunnel carved out beneath one of the city's main streets. At the end of the tunnel there is an underground station where passengers pass through glass doors right into the store itself.

This 'Shopper's Tramway' exists at Fort Worth. It serves Leonard's department store and was opened as recently as 1963. To work the service five PCC's were purchased second-hand from Washington and were extensively rebuilt with shining aluminium and such luxuries as air-conditioning.

But if you want to see the most modern tramway in the world you should go to Gothenburg in Sweden. You might not think there was anything special about the centre of the town, where the trams run along the streets in the normal way, but in the suburbs the picture is quite a revelation.

The routes have been extended into new suburbs in all directions, and the layout is just like a railway worked by tramcars. The lines are laid on their own right of way and are so planned that road crossings are avoided. On the route to Biskopsgarden, for example, there is a stretch of nearly five miles without a single crossing where delays could occur. Where necessary, tunnels have been blasted out of solid rock, and substantial stations have been built.

The cars that work on this impressive system are enormous by the standards of any other town. They are blue and white, streamlined, and have wide double seats on each side of the gangway with plenty of standing room as well. On some routes two-car trains run to a junction in the suburbs; the two vehicles then uncouple and the first goes off along one route while in the second the conductor becomes the driver and takes his car along the other route. In the reverse direction the coupling-up is accomplished equally smartly.

Gothenburg pioneered the electronically-controlled tramcar, with the result that the fleet is now equipped with anti-wheel-slip contrivances for safe acceleration and braking, as well as an automatic acceleration device which is a tiny computer in itself.

What is the most fascinating aspect of this space-age tram strikes you as soon as you get on. You notice curious undertones of conversation going on around the driver, although apparently no one is talking. The secret is the short-wave radio that is fitted to every bus and tram to keep it in contact with the central control point. By this means any traffic hold-ups or irregularities can be reported instantly and immediate action can be taken to prevent disturbances developing in the service.